REDEMPTOR HOMINIS

St. Pope John Paul II

Papal Writings of John Paul II

Volume 2

Henderson Publishing

Copyright ©2024 by Henderson Publishing.
Published June 2024.
Version: 1.0.
ISBN: 978-1-964170-00-8

If you have a question or have found an error concerning this manuscript, please email: lenouvelesprit@gmail.com
The Church documents presented here are used with permission by ©Libreria Editrice Vaticana.

Book cover designed by Christian Caudill.
Book designed by Jeremy Hausotter.
Front cover image used with permission by Rob Croes under the Creative Commons Attribution 4.0 International license.
Image Source: Wikimedia Commons.
URL: https://commons.wikimedia.org/wiki/File:
JohannesPaulusSimonis1985.2_(cropped).jpg
This book is typeset in Garamond Libre.

Henderson Publishing | San Antonio, Texas

Table of Contents

Redemptor Hominis

At the Beginning of His Pontifical Ministry
March 4, 1979

Venerable Brothers, and dear Sons and Daughters
Greetings and the Apostolic Blessing.

I.   Inheritance

1.   *At the close of the second Millennium*

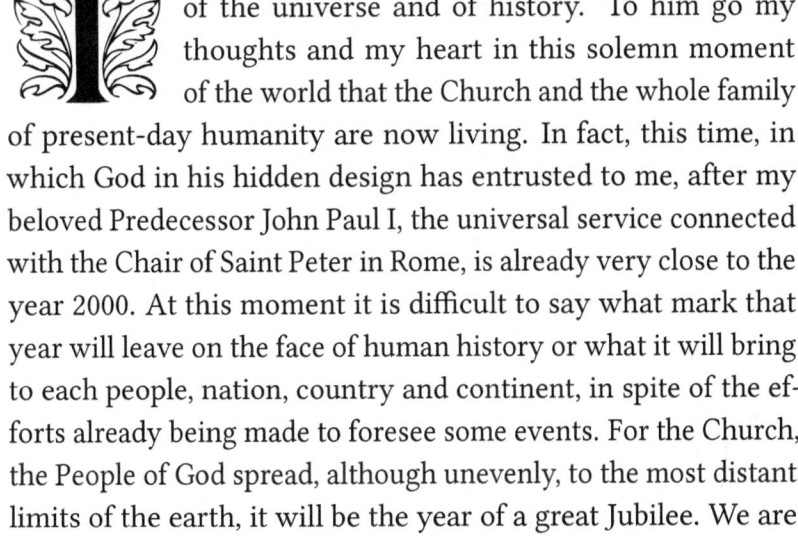

THE REDEEMER OF MAN, Jesus Christ, is the centre of the universe and of history. To him go my thoughts and my heart in this solemn moment of the world that the Church and the whole family of present-day humanity are now living. In fact, this time, in which God in his hidden design has entrusted to me, after my beloved Predecessor John Paul I, the universal service connected with the Chair of Saint Peter in Rome, is already very close to the year 2000. At this moment it is difficult to say what mark that year will leave on the face of human history or what it will bring to each people, nation, country and continent, in spite of the efforts already being made to foresee some events. For the Church, the People of God spread, although unevenly, to the most distant limits of the earth, it will be the year of a great Jubilee. We are already approaching that date, which, without prejudice to all the corrections imposed by chronological exactitude, will recall and reawaken in us in a special way our awareness of the key truth of faith which Saint John expressed at the beginning of his Gospel: "The Word became flesh and dwelt among us",[1] and elsewhere: "God so loved the world that he gave his only Son, that whoever believes in him should not perish but have eternal life".[2]

We also are in a certain way in a season of a new Advent, a season of expectation: "In many and various ways God spoke of old to our fathers by the prophets; but in these last days he has spoken to us by a Son . . .",[3] by the Son, his Word, who became man and was born of the Virgin Mary. This act of redemption marked the high point of the history of man within God's loving plan. God entered the history of humanity and, as a man, became an actor in that history, one of the thousands of millions of human beings but at the same time Unique! Through the Incarnation God gave human life the dimension that he intended man to have from his first beginning; he has granted that dimension definitively—in the way that is peculiar to him alone, in keeping with his eternal love and mercy, with the full freedom of God—and he has granted it also with the bounty that enables us, in considering the original sin and the whole history of the sins of humanity, and in considering the errors of the human intellect, will and heart, to repeat with amazement the words of the Sacred Liturgy: "O happy fault . . . which gained us so great a Redeemer!"[4]

---

[1]   Jn 1:14.

[2]   Jn 3:16.

[3]   Heb 1:1-2.

[4]   *Exsultet* at the Easter Vigil.

2. *The first words of the new Pontificate*

It was to Christ the Redeemer that my feelings and my thoughts were directed on 16 October of last year, when, after the canonical election, I was asked: "Do you accept?" I then replied: "With obedience in faith to Christ, my Lord, and with trust in the Mother of Christ and of the Church, in spite of the great difficulties, I accept". Today I wish to make that reply known publicly to all without exception, thus showing that there is a link between the first fundamental truth of the Incarnation, already mentioned, and the ministry that, with my acceptance of my election as Bishop of Rome and Successor of the Apostle Peter, has become my specific duty in his See.

I chose the same names that were chosen by my beloved Predecessor John Paul I. Indeed, as soon as he announced to the Sacred College on 26 August 1978 that he wished to be called John Paul—such a double name being unprecedented in the history of the Papacy—I saw in it a clear presage of grace for the new pontificate. Since that pontificate lasted barely 33 days, it falls to me not only to continue it but in a certain sense to take it up again at the same starting point. This is confirmed by my choice of these two names. By following the example of my venerable Predecessor in choosing them, I wish like him to express my love for the unique inheritance left to the Church by Popes John XXIII and Paul VI and my personal readiness to develop that inheritance with God's help.

Through these two names and two pontificates I am linked with the whole tradition of the Apostolic See and with all my Predecessors in the expanse of the twentieth century and of the preceding centuries. I am connected, through one after another of the various ages back to the most remote, with the line of the mission and ministry that confers on Peter's See an altogether special place in the Church. John XXIII and Paul VI are a stage to which I wish to refer directly as a threshold from which I intend to continue, in a certain sense together with John Paul I, into the future, letting myself be guided by unlimited trust in and obedience to the Spirit that Christ promised and sent to his Church. On the night before he suffered he said to his apostles: "It is to your advantage that I go away, for if I do not go away, the Counsellor will not come to you; but if I go, I will send him to you".[5] "When the Counsellor comes, whom I shall send to you from the Father, even the Spirit of truth, who proceeds from the Father, he will bear witness to me; and you also are witnesses, because you have been with me from the beginning".[6] "When the Spirit of truth comes, he will guide you into all the truth; for he will not speak on his own authority, but whatever he hears he will speak, and he will declare to you the things that are to come".[7]

3. *Trust in the Spirit of Truth and of Love*

Entrusting myself fully to the Spirit of truth, therefore, I am entering into the rich inheritance of the recent pontificates. This inheritance has struck deep roots in the awareness of the Church in an utterly new way, quite unknown previously, thanks to the Second Vatican Council, which John XXIII convened and opened and which was later successfully concluded and perseveringly put into effect by Paul VI, whose activity I was myself able to watch from close at hand. I was constantly amazed at his profound wisdom and his courage and also by his constancy and

---

[5]   Jn 16:7.

[6]   Jn 15:26-27.

[7]   Jn 16:13.

patience in the difficult postconciliar period of his pontificate. As helmsman of the Church, the bark of Peter, he knew how to preserve a providential tranquillity and balance even in the most critical moments, when the Church seemed to be shaken from within, and he always maintained unhesitating hope in the Church's solidity. What the Spirit said to the Church through the Council of our time, what the Spirit says in this Church to all the Churches[8] cannot lead to anything else—in spite of momentary uneasinesses—but still more mature solidity of the whole People of God, aware of their salvific mission.

Paul VI selected this present-day consciousness of the Church as the first theme in his fundamental Encyclical beginning with the words *Ecclesiam Suam.* Let me refer first of all to this Encyclical and link myself with it in this first document that, so to speak, inaugurates the present pontificate. The Church's consciousness, enlightened and supported by the Holy Spirit and fathoming more and more deeply both her divine mystery and her human mission, and even her human weaknesses-this consciousness is and must remain the first source of the Church's love, as love in turn helps to strengthen and deepen her consciousness. Paul VI left us a witness of such an extremely acute consciousness of the Church. Through the many things, often causing suffering, that went to make up his pontificate he taught us intrepid love for the Church, which is, as the Council states, a "sacrament or sign and means of intimate union with God, and of the unity of all mankind".[9]

---

[8] Cf. Rev 2:7.
[9] Vatican Council II: Dogmatic Constitution on the Church *Lumen Gentium*, 1: AAS 57 (1965) 5.

4.　*Reference to Paul VI's first Encyclical*

Precisely for this reason, the Church's consciousness must go with universal openness, in order that all may be able to find in her "the unsearchable riches of Christ"[10] spoken of by the Apostle of the Gentiles. Such openness, organically joined with the awareness of her own nature and certainty of her own truth, of which Christ said: "The word which you hear is not mine but the Father's who sent me",[11] is what gives the Church her apostolic, or in other words her missionary, dynamism, professing and proclaiming in its integrity the whole of the truth transmitted by Christ. At the same time she must carry on the dialogue that Paul VI, in his Encyclical *Ecclesiam Suam* called "the dialogue of salvation", distinguishing with precision the various circles within which it was to be carried on.[12] In referring today to this document that gave the programme of Paul VI's pontificate, I keep thanking God that this great Predecessor of mine, who was also truly my father, knew how to display *ad extra*, externally, the true countenance of the Church, in spite of the various internal weaknesses that affected her in the postconciliar period. In this way much of the human family has become, it seems, more aware, in all humanity's various spheres of existence, of how really necessary the Church of Christ, her mission and her service are to humanity. At times this awareness has proved stronger than the various critical attitudes attacking *ab intra*, internally, the Church, her institutions and structures, and ecclesiastics and their activities. This growing criticism was certainly due to various causes and we are furthermore sure that it was not

---

[10]　Eph 3:8.

[11]　Jn 14:24.

[12]　Pope Paul VI: Encyclical Letter *Ecclesiam Suam:* AAS 56 (1964) 650ff.

always without sincere love for the Church. Undoubtedly one of the tendencies it displayed was to overcome what has been called triumphalism, about which there was frequent discussion during the Council. While it is right that, in accordance with the example of her Master, who is "humble in heart",[13] the Church also should have humility as her foundation, that she should have a critical sense with regard to all that goes to make up her human character and activity, and that she should always be very demanding on herself, nevertheless criticism too should have its just limits. Otherwise it ceases to be constructive and does not reveal truth, love and thankfulness for the grace in which we become sharers principally and fully in and through the Church. Furthermore such criticism does not express an attitude of service but rather a wish to direct the opinion of others in accordance with one's own, which is at times spread abroad in too thoughtless a manner.

Gratitude is due to Paul VI because, while respecting every particle of truth contained in the various human opinions, he preserved at the same time the providential balance of the bark's helmsman.[14] The Church that I—through John Paul I—have had

---

[13] Mt 11:29.

[14] Mention must be made here of the salient documents of the pontificate of Paul VI, some of which were spoken of by himself in his address during Mass on the Solemnity of the Holy Apostles Peter and Paul in 1978: Encyclical *Ecclesiam Suam:* AAS 56 (1964) 609-659; Apostolic Letter *Investigabiles Divitias Christi:* AAS 57 (1965) 298-301; Encyclical *Sacerdotalis Caelibatus:* AAS 59 (1967) 657-697; Solemn Profession of Faith: AAS 60 (1968) 433-445; Encyclical *Humanae Vitae:* AAS 60 (1968) 481-503; Apostolic Exhortation *Quinque Iam Anni:* AAS 63 (1971) 97-106; Apostolic Exhortation *Evangelica Testificatio:* AAS 63 (1971) 497-535; Apostolic Exhortation *Paterna cum Benevolentia:* AAS 67 (1975) 5-23; Apostolic Exhortation *Gaudete in Domino:* AAS 67 (1975) 289-322; Apostolic Exhortation *Evangelii Nuntiandi:* AAS 68 (1976) 5-76.

entrusted to me almost immediately after him is admittedly not free of internal difficulties and tension. At the same time, however, she is internally more strengthened against the excesses of self-criticism: she can be said to be more critical with regard to the various thoughtless criticisms, more resistent with respect to the various "novelties", more mature in her spirit of discerning, better able to bring out of her everlasting treasure "what is new and what is old",[15] more intent on her own mystery, and because of all that more serviceable for her mission of salvation for all: God "desires all men to be saved and to come to the knowledge of the truth".[16]

5.   *Collegiality and apostolate*

In spite of all appearances, the Church is now more united in the fellowship of service and in the awareness of apostolate. This unity springs from the principle of collegiality, mentioned by the Second Vatican Council. Christ himself made this principle a living part of the apostolic College of the Twelve with Peter at their head, and he is continuously renewing it in the College of the Bishops, which is growing more and more over all the earth, remaining united with and under the guidance of the Successor of Saint Peter. The Council did more than mention the principle of collegiality: it gave it immense new life, by— among other things—expressing the wish for a permanent organ of collegiality, which Paul VI founded by setting up the Synod of the Bishops, whose activity not only gave a new dimension to his pontificate but was also later clearly reflected in the pontificate of John Paul I and that of his unworthy Successor from the day they began.

---

[15]   Mt 13:52.

[16]   1 Tim 2:4.

The principle of collegiality showed itself particularly relevant in the difficult postconciliar period, when the shared unanimous position of the College of the Bishops—which displayed, chiefly through the Synod, its union with Peter's Successor—helped to dissipate doubts and at the same time indicated the correct ways for renewing the Church in her universal dimension. Indeed, the Synod was the source, among other things, of that essential momentum for evangelization that found expression in the Apostolic Exhortation *Evangelii Nuntiandi*,[17] which was so joyously welcomed as a programme for renewal which was both apostolic and also pastoral. The same line was followed in the work of the last ordinary session of the Synod of the Bishops, held about a year before the death of Pope Paul VI and dedicated, as is known, to catechesis. The results of this work have still to be arranged and enunciated by the Apostolic See.

As we are dealing with the evident development of the forms in which episcopal collegiality is expressed, mention must be made at least of the process of consolidation of National Episcopal Conferences throughout the Church and of other collegial structures of an international or continental character. Referring also to the centuries old tradition of the Church, attention should be directed to the activity of the various diocesan, provincial and national Synods. It was the Council's idea, an idea consistently put into practice by Paul VI, that structures of this kind, with their centuries of trial by the Church, and the other forms of collegial collaboration by Bishops, such as the metropolitan structure—not to mention each individual diocese—should pulsate in full awareness of their own identity and, at the same time, of their own originality within the universal unity of the

---

[17] Pope Paul VI: Apostolic Exhortation *Evangelii Nuntiandi:* AAS 68 (1976) 5-76.

Church. The same spirit of collaboration and shared responsibility is spreading among priests also, as is confirmed by the many Councils of Priests that have sprung up since the Council. That spirit has extended also among the laity, not only strengthening the already existing organizations for lay apostolate but also creating new ones that often have a different outline and excellent dynamism. Furthermore, lay people conscious of their responsibility for the Church have willingly committed themselves to collaborating with the Pastors and with the representatives of the Institutes of consecrated life, in the spheres of the diocesan Synods and of the pastoral Councils in the parishes and dioceses.

I must keep all this in mind at the beginning of my pontificate as a reason for giving thanks to God, for warmly encouraging all my brothers and sisters and for recalling with heartfelt gratitude the work of the Second Vatican Council and my great Predecessors, who set in motion this new surge of life for the Church, a movement that is much stronger than the symptoms of doubt, collapse and crisis.

6.   *The road to Christian unity*

What shall I say of all the initiatives that have sprung from the new ecumenical orientation? The unforgettable Pope John XXIII set out the problem of Christian unity with evangelical clarity as a simple consequence of the will of Jesus Christ himself, our Master, the will that Jesus stated on several occasions but to which he gave expression in a special way in his prayer in the Upper Room the night before he died: "I pray . . . Father . . . that they may all be one".[18] The Second Vatican Council responded concisely to this requirement with its Decree on ecumenism.

---

[18]   Jn 17:21; cf. 17:11, 22-23; 10:16; Lk 9:49, 50, 54.

Pope Paul VI, availing himself of the activities of the Secretariat for Promoting Christian Unity, began the first difficult steps on the road to the attainment of that unity. Have we gone far along that road? Without wishing to give a detailed reply, we can say that we have made real and important advances. And one thing is certain: we have worked with perseverance and consistency, and the representatives of other Christian Churches and Communities have also committed themselves together with us, for which we are heartily grateful to them. It is also certain that in the present historical situation of Christianity and the world the only possibility we see of fulfilling the Church's universal mission, with regard to ecumenical questions, is that of seeking sincerely, perseveringly, humbly and also courageously the ways of drawing closer and of union. Pope Paul VI gave us his personal example for this. We must therefore seek unity without being discouraged at the difficulties that can appear or accumulate along that road; otherwise we would be unfaithful to the word of Christ, we would fail to accomplish his testament. Have we the right to run this risk?

There are people who in the face of the difficulties or because they consider that the first ecumenical endeavours have brought negative results would have liked to turn back. Some even express the opinion that these efforts are harmful to the cause of the Gospel, are leading to a further rupture in the Church, are causing confusion of ideas in questions of faith and morals and are ending up with a specific indifferentism. It is perhaps a good thing that the spokesmen for these opinions should express their fears. However, in this respect also, correct limits must be maintained. It is obvious that this new stage in the Church's life demands of us a faith that is particularly aware, profound and responsible. True ecumenical activity means openness, drawing

closer, availability for dialogue, and a shared investigation of
the truth in the full evangelical and Christian sense; but in no
way does it or can it mean giving up or in any way diminish-
ing the treasures of divine truth that the Church has constantly
confessed and taught. To all who, for whatever motive, would
wish to dissuade the Church from seeking the universal unity
of Christians the question must once again be put: Have we the
right not to do it? Can we fail to have trust—in spite of all human
weakness and all the faults of past centuries—in our Lord's grace
as revealed recently through what the Holy Spirit said and we
heard during the Council? If we were to do so, we would deny
the truth concerning ourselves that was so eloquently expressed
by the Apostle: "By the grace of God I am what I am, and his
grace towards me was not in vain".[19]

What we have just said must also be applied—although in
another way and with the due differences—to activity for coming
closer together with the representatives of the non-Christian religions, an activity expressed through dialogue, contacts, prayer in
common, investigation of the treasures of human spirituality, in
which, as we know well, the members of these religions also are
not lacking. Does it not sometimes happen that the firm belief
of the followers of the non-Christian religions—a belief that is
also an effect of the Spirit of truth operating outside the visible
confines of the Mystical Body—can make Christians ashamed
at being often themselves so disposed to doubt concerning the
truths revealed by God and proclaimed by the Church and so
prone to relax moral principles and open the way to ethical
permissiveness. It is a noble thing to have a predisposition for
understanding every person, analyzing every system and recog-

---

[19] 1 Cor 15:10.

nizing what is right; this does not at all mean losing certitude about one's own faith[20] or weakening the principles of morality, the lack of which will soon make itself felt in the life of whole societies, with deplorable consequences besides.

II.   The Mystery of the Redemption

7.   *Within the Mystery of Christ*

While the ways on which the Council of this century has set the Church going, ways indicated by the late Pope Paul VI in his first Encyclical, will continue to be for a long time the ways that all of us must follow, we can at the same time rightly ask at this new stage: How, in what manner should we continue? What should we do, in order that this new advent of the Church connected with the approaching end of the second millennium may bring us closer to him whom Sacred Scripture calls "Everlasting Father", *Pater futuri saeculi?*[21]   This is the fundamental question that the new Pope must put to himself on accepting in a spirit of obedience in faith the call corresponding to the command that Christ gave Peter several times: "Feed my lambs",[22] meaning: Be the shepherd of my sheepfold, and again: "And when you have turned again, strengthen your brethren".[23]

To this question, dear Brothers, sons and daughters, a fundamental and essential response must be given. Our response must be: Our spirit is set in one direction, the only direction for our intellect, will and heart is towards Christ our Redeemer,

---

[20] Cf. Vatican Council I: Dogmatic Constitution *Dei Filius*, Cap. III *De fide*, can. 6: *Conciliorum Oecumenicorum Decreta*, Ed. Istituto per le Scienze Religiose, Bologna 1973 3, p. 811.

[21] Is 9:6.

[22] Jn 21:15.

[23] Lk 22:32.

towards Christ, the Redeemer of man. We wish to look towards him—because there is salvation in no one else but him, the Son of God—repeating what Peter said: "Lord, to whom shall we go? You have the words of eternal life".[24]

Through the Church's consciousness, which the Council considerably developed, through all levels of this self-awareness, and through all the fields of activity in which the Church expresses, finds and confirms herself, we must constantly aim at him "who is the head",[25] "through whom are all things and through whom we exist",[26] who is both "the way, and the truth"[27] and "the resurrection and the life",[28] seeing whom, we see the Father,[29] and who had to go away from us[30]—that is, by his death on the Cross and then by his Ascension into heaven—in order that the Counsellor should come to us and should keep coming to us as the Spirit of truth.[31] In him are "all the treasures of wisdom and knowledge",[32] and the Church is his Body.[33] "By her relationship with Christ, the Church is a kind of sacrament or sign and means of intimate union with God, and of the unity of all mankind",[34] and the source of this is he, he himself, he the Redeemer.

The Church does not cease to listen to his words. She rereads them continually. With the greatest devotion she reconstructs

---

[24] Jn 6:68; cf. Acts 4:8-12.

[25] Cf. Eph 1:10, 22; 4:25; Col 1:18.

[26] 1 Cor 8:6; cf. Col 1:17.

[27] Jn 14:6.

[28] Jn 11:25.

[29] Cf. Jn 14:9.

[30] Cf. Jn 16:7.

[31] Cf. Jn 16:7, 13.

[32] Col 2:3.

[33] Cf. Rom 12:5; 1 Cor 6:15; 10:17; 12:12, 27; Eph 1:23; 2:16; 4:4; Col 1:24; 3:15.

[34] Vatican Council II: Dogmatic Constitution on the Church *Lumen Gentium*, 1: AAS 57 (1965) 5.

every detail of his life. These words are listened to also by non-Christians. The life of Christ speaks, also, to many who are not capable of repeating with Peter: "You are the Christ, the Son of the living God".[35] He, the Son of the living God, speaks to people also as Man: it is his life that speaks, his humanity, his fidelity to the truth, his all-embracing love. Furthermore, his death on the Cross speaks—that is to say—the inscrutable depth of his suffering and abandonment. The Church never ceases to relive his death on the Cross and his Resurrection, which constitute the content of the Church's daily life. Indeed, it is by the command of Christ himself, her Master, that the Church unceasingly celebrates the Eucharist, finding in it the "fountain of life and holiness",[36] the efficacious sign of grace and reconciliation with God, and the pledge of eternal life. The Church lives his mystery, draws unwearyingly from it and continually seeks ways of bringing this mystery of her Master and Lord to humanity—to the peoples, the nations, the succeeding generations, and every individual human being—as if she were ever repeating, as the Apostle did: "For I decided to know nothing among you except Jesus Christ and him crucified".[37] The Church stays within the sphere of the mystery of the Redemption, which has become the fundamental principle of her life and mission.

8.   *Redemption as a new creation*

The Redeemer of the world! In him has been revealed in a new and more wonderful way the fundamental truth concerning creation to which the Book of Genesis gives witness when it

---

[35] Mt 16:16.

[36] Cf. Litany of the Sacred Heart.

[37] 1 Cor 2:2.

repeats several times: "God saw that it was good".[38] The good has its source in Wisdom and Love. In Jesus Christ the visible world which God created for man[39]—the world that, when sin entered, "was subjected to futility"[40]—recovers again its original link with the divine source of Wisdom and Love. Indeed, "God so loved the world that he gave his only Son".[41] As this link was broken in the man Adam, so in the Man Christ it was reforged.[42] Are we of the twentieth century not convinced of the over poweringly eloquent words of the Apostle of the Gentiles concerning the "creation (that) has been groaning in travail together until now"[43] and "waits with eager longing for the revelation of the sons of God",[44] the creation that "was subjected to futility"? Does not the previously unknown immense progress—which has taken place especially in the course of this century—in the field of man's dominion over the world itself reveal—to a previously unknown degree—that manifold subjection "to futility"? It is enough to recall certain phenomena, such as the threat of pollution of the natural environment in areas of rapid industrialization, or the armed conflicts continually breaking out over and over again, or the prospectives of self-destruction through the use of atomic, hydrogen, neutron and similar weapons, or the lack of respect for the life of the unborn. The world of the new age, the world of space flights, the world of the previously unattained conquests

---

[38] Cf. Gen 1 *passim*.

[39] Cf. Gen 1:26-30.

[40] Rom . 8: 20; cf . 8:19-22; Vatican Council II: Pastoral Constitution on the Church in the Modern World *Gaudium et Spes*, 2, 13: AAS 58 (1966) 1026, 1034-1035.

[41] Jn 3:16.

[42] Cf. Rom 5:12-21.

[43] Rom 8:22.

[44] Rom 8:19.

of science and technology—is it not also the world "groaning in travail"[45] that "waits with eager longing for the revealing of the sons of God"?[46]

In its penetrating analysis of "the modern world", the Second Vatican Council reached that most important point of the visible world that is man, by penetrating like Christ the depth of human consciousness and by making contact with the inward mystery of man, which in Biblical and non-Biblical language is expressed by the word "heart". Christ, the Redeemer of the world, is the one who penetrated in a unique unrepeatable way into the mystery of man and entered his "heart". Rightly therefore does the Second Vatican Council teach: "The truth is that only in the mystery of the Incarnate Word does the mystery of man take on light. For Adam, the first man, was a type of him who was to come (Rom 5:14), Christ the Lord. Christ the new Adam, in the very revelation of the mystery of the Father and of his love, *fully reveals man to himself* and brings to light his most high calling". And the Council continues: "He who is the 'image of the invisible God' (Col 1:15), is himself the perfect man who has restored in the children of Adam that likeness to God which had been disfigured ever since the first sin. Human nature, by the very fact that is was assumed, not absorbed, in him, has been raised in us also to a dignity beyond compare. For, by his Incarnation, he, the son of God, *in a certain way united himself with each man.* He worked with human hands, he thought with a human mind. He acted with a human will, and with a human heart he loved. Born of the Virgin Mary, he has truly been made one of us, like to us in all things except sin",[47] he, the Redeemer of man.

---

[45] Rom 8:22.

[46] Rom 8:19.

[47] Vatican Council II: Pastoral Constitution on the Church in the Modern

9.   *The divine dimension of the mystery of the Redemption*

As we reflect again on this stupendous text from the Council's teaching, we do not forget even for a moment that Jesus Christ, the Son of the living God, become our reconciliation with the Father.[48] He it was, and he alone, who satisfied the Father's eternal love, that fatherhood that from the beginning found expression in creating the world, giving man all the riches of creation, and making him "little less than God",[49] in that he was created "in the image and after the likeness of God".[50] He and he alone also satisfied that fatherhood of God and that love which man in a way rejected by breaking the first Covenant[51] and the later covenants that God "again and again offered to man".[52] The redemption of the world—this tremendous mystery of love in which creation is renewed—[53] is, at its deepest root, the fullness of justice in a human Heart—the Heart of the First-born Son—in order that it may become justice in the hearts of many human beings, predestined from eternity in the Firstborn Son to be children of God[54] and called to grace, called to love. The Cross on Calvary, through which Jesus Christ—a Man, the Son of the Virgin Mary, thought to be the son of Joseph of Nazareth— "leaves" this world, is also a fresh manifestation of the eternal fatherhood of God, who in him draws near again to humanity, to

---

World *Gaudium et Spes*, 22: AAS 58 (1966) 1042-1043.

[48]   Rom 5:11; Col 1:20.

[49]   Ps 8:6.

[50]   Cf. Gn 1:26.

[51]   Cf. Gn 3:6-13.

[52]   Cf. Eucharistic Prayer IV.

[53]   Cf. Vatican Council II: Pastoral Constitution on the Church in the Modern World *Gaudium et Spes*, 37: AAS 58 (1966) 1054-1055; Dogmatic Constitution on the Church *Lumen Gentium*, 48: AAS 57 (1965) 53-54.

[54]   Cf. Rom 8:29-30; Eph 1:8.

each human being, giving him the thrice holy "Spirit of truth".[55]

This revelation of the Father and outpouring of the Holy Spirit, which stamp an indelible seal on the mystery of the Redemption, explain the meaning of the Cross and death of Christ. The God of creation is revealed as the God of redemption, as the God who is "faithful to himself",[56] and faithful to his love for man and the world, which he revealed on the day of creation. His is a love that does not draw back before anything that justice requires in him. Therefore "for our sake (God) made him (the Son) to be sin who knew no sin".[57] If he "made to be sin" him who was without any sin whatever, it was to reveal the love that is always greater than the whole of creation, the love that is he himself, since "God is love".[58] Above all, love is greater than sin, than weakness, than the "futility of creation",[59] it is stronger than death; it is a love always ready to raise up and forgive, always ready to go to meet the prodigal son,[60] always looking for "the revealing of the sons of God",[61] who are called to the glory that is to be revealed.[62] This revelation of love is also described as mercy;[63] and in man's history this revelation of love and mercy has taken a form and a name: that of Jesus Christ.

---

[55] Cf. Jn 16:13.
[56] Cf. 1 Thes 5:24.
[57] 2 Cor 5:21; cf. Gal 3:13.
[58] 1 Jn 4:8, 16.
[59] Cf. Rom 8:20.
[60] Cf. Lk 15:11-32.
[61] Rom 8:19.
[62] Cf. Rom 8:18.
[63] Cf. St. Thomas, *Summa Theol.*, III, q. 46, a. 1, ad 3.

10.   *The human dimension of the mystery of the Redemption*

Man cannot live without love. He remains a being that is incomprehensible for himself, his life is senseless, if love is not revealed to him, if he does not encounter love, if he does not experience it and make it his own, if he does not participate intimately in it. This, as has already been said, is why Christ the Redeemer "fully reveals man to himself". If we may use the expression, this is the human dimension of the mystery of the Redemption. In this dimension man finds again the greatness, dignity and value that belong to his humanity. In the mystery of the Redemption man becomes newly "expressed" and, in a way, is newly created. He is newly created! "There is neither Jew nor Greek, there is neither slave nor free, there is neither male nor female; for you are all one in Christ Jesus".[64] The man who wishes to understand himself thoroughly—and not just in accordance with immediate, partial, often superficial, and even illusory standards and measures of his being—he must with his unrest, uncertainty and even his weakness and sinfulness, with his life and death, draw near to Christ. He must, so to speak, enter into him with all his own self, he must "appropriate" and assimilate the whole of the reality of the Incarnation and Redemption in order to find himself. If this profound process takes place within him, he then bears fruit not only of adoration of God but also of deep wonder at himself. How precious must man be in the eyes of the Creator, if he "gained so great a Redeemer",[65] and if God "gave his only Son "in order that man "should not perish but have eternal life".[66]

In reality, the name for that deep amazement at man's worth

---

[64]   Gal 3:28.

[65]   *Exsultet* at the Easter Vigil.

[66]   Cf. Jn 3:16.

and dignity is the Gospel, that is to say: the Good News. It is also called Christianity. This amazement determines the Church's mission in the world and, perhaps even more so, "in the modern world". This amazement, which is also a conviction and a certitude—at its deepest root it is the certainty of faith, but in a hidden and mysterious way it vivifies every aspect of authentic humanism—is closely connected with Christ. It also fixes Christ's place—so to speak, his particular right of citizenship—in the history of man and mankind. Unceasingly contemplating the whole of Christ's mystery, the Church knows with all the certainty of faith that the Redemption that took place through the Cross has definitively restored his dignity to man and given back meaning to his life in the world, a meaning that was lost to a considerable extent because of sin. And for that reason, the Redemption was accomplished in the paschal mystery, leading through the Cross and death to Resurrection.

The Church's fundamental function in every age and particularly in ours is to direct man's gaze, to point the awareness and experience of the whole of humanity towards the mystery of God, to help all men to be familiar with the profundity of the Redemption taking place in Christ Jesus. At the same time man's deepest sphere is involved—we mean the sphere of human hearts, consciences and events.

11.   *The mystery of Christ as the basis of the Church's mission and of Christianity*

The Second Vatican Council did immense work to form that full and universal awareness by the Church of which Pope Paul VI wrote in his first Encyclical. This awareness—or rather self-awareness—by the Church is formed a "in dialogue"; and before this dialogue becomes a conversation, attention must be directed to "the other", that is to say: the person with whom we wish to speak. The Ecumenical Council gave a fundamental impulse to forming the Church's self-awareness by so adequately and competently presenting to us a view of the terrestrial globe as a map of various religions. It showed furthermore that this map of the world's religions has superimposed on it, in previously unknown layers typical of our time, the phenomenon of atheism in its various forms, beginning with the atheism that is programmed, organized and structured as a political system.

With regard to religion, what is dealt with is in the first place religion as a universal phenomenon linked with man's history from the beginning, then the various non-Christian religions, and finally Christianity itself. The Council document on non-Christian religions, in particular, is filled with deep esteem for the great spiritual values, indeed for the primacy of the spiritual, which in the life of mankind finds expression in religion and then in morality, with direct effects on the whole of culture. The Fathers of the Church rightly saw in the various religions as it were so many reflections of the one truth, "seeds of the Word",[67] attesting that, though the routes taken may be different, there is but a single goal to which is directed the deepest aspiration of the human spirit as expressed in its quest for God and also in its quest, through its tending towards God, for the full dimension of its humanity, or in other words for the full meaning of human life. The Council gave particular attention to the Jewish religion,

---

[67] Cf. St. Justin, *I Apologia*, 46, 1-4; *II Apologia*, 7 (8), 1-4; 10, 1-3; 13, 3-4; *Florilegium Patristicum*, II, Bonn 1911 2, pp. 81, 125, 129, 133; Clement of Alexandria, *Stromata*, I, 19, 91 and 94: *Sources Chrétiennes*, 30, pp. 117-118; 119-120; Vatican Council II, Decree on the Church's Missionary Activity *Ad Gentes*, 11: AAS 58 (1966) 960; Dogmatic Constitution on the Church *Lumen Gentium*, 17: AAS 57 (1965) 21.

recalling the great spiritual heritage common to Christians and Jews. It also expressed its esteem for the believers of Islam, whose faith also looks to Abraham.[68]

The opening made by the Second Vatican Council has enabled the Church and all Christians to reach a more complete awareness of the mystery of Christ, "the mystery hidden for ages"[69] in God, to be revealed in time in the Man Jesus Christ, and to be revealed continually in every time. In Christ and through Christ God has revealed himself fully to mankind and has definitively drawn close to it; at the same time, in Christ and through Christ man has acquired full awareness of his dignity, of the heights to which he is raised, of the surpassing worth of his own humanity, and of the meaning of his existence.

All of us who are Christ's followers must therefore meet and unite around him. This unity in the various fields of the life, tradition, structures and discipline of the individual Christian Churches and ecclesial Communities cannot be brought about without effective work aimed at getting to know each other and removing the obstacles blocking the way to perfect unity. However, we can and must immediately reach and display to the world our unity in proclaiming the mystery of Christ, in revealing the divine dimension and also the human dimension of the Redemption, and in struggling with unwearying perseverance for the dignity that each human being has reached and can continually reach in Christ, namely the dignity of both the grace of divine adoption and the inner truth of humanity, a truth which—if in the common awareness of the modern world it has been given such fundamental importance—for us is still clearer

---

[68] Cf. Vatican Council II: Declaration on the Church's Relations with Non-Christian Religions *Nostra Aetate*, 3-4: AAS 58 (1966) 741-743.

[69] Col 1:26.

in the light of the reality that is Jesus Christ.

Jesus Christ is the stable principle and fixed centre of the mission that God himself has entrusted to man. We must all share in this mission and concentrate all our forces on it, since it is more necessary than ever for modern mankind. If this mission seems to encounter greater opposition nowadays than ever before, this shows that today it is more necessary than ever and, in spite of the opposition, more awaited than ever. Here we touch indirectly on the mystery of the divine "economy" which linked salvation and grace with the Cross. It was not without reason that Christ said that "the kingdom of heaven has suffered violence, and men of violence take it by force"[70] and moreover that "the children of this world are more astute . . . than are the children of light".[71] We gladly accept this rebuke, that we may be like those "violent people of God "that we have so often seen in the history of the Church and still see today, and that we may consciously join in the great mission of revealing Christ to the world, helping each person to find himself in Christ, and helping the contemporary generations of our brothers and sisters, the peoples, nations, States, mankind, developing countries and countries of opulence—in short, helping everyone to get to know "the unsearchable riches of Christ",[72] since these riches are for every individual and are everybody's property.

12.   *The Church's mission and human freedom*

In this unity in mission, which is decided principally by Christ himself, all Christians must find what already unites them, even before their full communion is achieved. This is apostolic and

---

[70] Mt 11:12.

[71] Lk 16:8.

[72] Eph 3:8.

missionary unity, missionary and apostolic unity. Thanks to this unity we can together come close to the magnificent heritage of the human spirit that has been manifested in all religions, as the Second Vatican Council's Declaration *Nostra Aetate* says.[73] It also enables us to approach all cultures, all ideological concepts, all people of good will. We approach them with the esteem, respect and discernment that since the time of the Apostles has marked the *missionary* attitude, the attitude *of the missionary.* Suffice it to mention Saint Paul and, for instance, his address in the Areopagus at Athens.[74] The *missionary* attitude always begins with a feeling of deep esteem for "what is in man",[75] for what man has himself. worked out in the depths of his spirit concerning the most profound and important problems. It is a question of respecting everything that has been brought about in him by the Spirit, which "blows where it wills".[76] The mission is never destruction, but instead is a taking up and fresh building, even if in practice there has not always been full correspondence with this high ideal. And we know well that the conversion that is begun by the mission is a work of grace, in which man must fully find himself again.

For this reason the Church in our time attaches great importance to all that is stated by the Second Vatican Council in its *Declaration on Religious Freedom*, both the first and the second part of the document.[77] We perceive intimately that the truth revealed to us by God imposes on us an obligation. We have,

---

[73] Cf. Vatican Council II: Declaration *Nostra Aetate*, 1-2: AAS 58 (1966) 740-741.

[74] Acts 17:22-31.

[75] Jn 2:26.

[76] Jn 3:8.

[77] Cf. AAS 58 (1966) 929-946.

in particular, a great sense of responsibility for this truth. By Christ's institution the Church is its guardian and teacher, having been endowed with a unique assistance of the Holy Spirit in order to guard and teach it in its most exact integrity.[78] In fulfilling this mission, we look towards Christ himself, the first evangelizer,[79] and also towards his Apostles, martyrs and confessors. The *Declaration on Religious Freedom* shows us convincingly that, when Christ and, after him, his Apostles proclaimed the truth that comes not from men but from God ("My teaching is not mine, but his who sent me",[80] that is the Father's), they preserved, while acting with their full force of spirit, a deep esteem for man, for his intellect, his will, his conscience and his freedom.[81] Thus the human person's dignity itself becomes part of the content of that proclamation, being included not necessarily in words but by an attitude towards it. This attitude seems to fit the special needs of our times. Since man's true freedom is not found in everything that the various systems and individuals see and propagate as freedom, the Church, because of her divine mission, becomes all the more the guardian of this freedom, which is the condition and basis for the human person's true dignity.

Jesus Christ meets the man of every age, including our own, with the same words: "You will know the truth, and the truth will make you free".[82] These words contain both a fundamental requirement and a warning: the requirement of an honest relationship with regard to truth as a condition for authentic

---

[78] Cf. Jn 14:26.

[79] Pope Paul VI: Apostolic Exhortation *Evangelii Nuntiandi*, 6: AAS 68 (1976) 9.

[80] Jn 7:16.

[81] Cf. AAS 58 (1966) 936-938.

[82] Jn 8:32.

freedom, and the warning to avoid every kind of illusory freedom, every superficial unilateral freedom, every freedom that fails to enter into the whole truth about man and the world. Today also, even after two thousand years, we see Christ as the one who brings man freedom based on truth, frees man from what curtails, diminishes and as it were breaks off this freedom at its root, in man's soul, his heart and his conscience. What a stupendous confirmation of this has been given and is still being given by those who, thanks to Christ and in Christ, have reached true freedom and have manifested it even in situations of external constraint!

When Jesus Christ himself appeared as a prisoner before Pilate's tribunal and was interrogated by him about the accusation made against him by the representatives of the Sanhedrin, did he not answer: "For this I was born, and for this I have come into the world, to bear witness to the truth"?[83] It was as if with these words spoken before the judge at the decisive moment he was once more confirming what he had said earlier: "You will know the truth, and the truth will make you free". In the course of so many centuries, of so many generations, from the time of the Apostles on, is it not often Jesus Christ himself that has made an appearance at the side of people judged for the sake of the truth? And has he not gone to death with people condemned for the sake of the truth? Does he ever cease to be the continuous spokesman and advocate for the person who lives "in spirit and truth"?[84] Just as he does not cease to be it before the Father, he is it also with regard to the history of man. And in her turn the Church, in spite of all the weaknesses that are part of her human history, does not cease to follow him who said: "The hour is

---

[83] Jn 18:37.
[84] Cf. Jn 4:23.

coming, and now is, when the true worshippers will worship the
Father in spirit and truth, for such the Father seeks to worship
him. God is spirit, and those who worship him must worship in
spirit and truth".[85]

III.   Redeemed Man and his Situation in the Modern World

13.   *Christ united himself with each man*

When we penetrate by means of the continually and rapidly
increasing experience of the human family into the mystery of
Jesus Christ, we understand with greater clarity that there is at
the basis of all these ways that the Church of our time must follow,
in accordance with the wisdom of Pope Paul VI,[86] one single way:
it is the way that has stood the test of centuries and it is also the
way of the future. Christ the Lord indicated this way especially,
when, as the Council teaches, "by his Incarnation, he, the Son
of God, in a certain way *united himself with each man*".[87] The
Church therefore sees its fundamental task in enabling that union
to be brought about and renewed continually. The Church wishes
to serve this single end: that each person may be able to find
Christ, in order that Christ may walk with each person the path of
life, with the power of the truth about man and the world that is
contained in the mystery of the Incarnation and the Redemption
and with the power of the love that is radiated by that truth.
Against a background of the ever increasing historical processes,
which seem at the present time to have results especially within

---

[85]   Jn 4:23-24.
[86]   Cf. Pope Paul VI: Encyclical *Ecclesiam Suam:* AAS 56 (1964) 609-659.
[87]   Vatican Council II: Pastoral Constitution on the Church in the Modern
World *Gaudium et Spes*, 22: AAS 58 (1966) 1042.

the spheres of various systems, ideological concepts of the world and regimes, Jesus Christ becomes, in a way, newly present, in spite of all his apparent absences, in spite of all the limitations of the presence and of the institutional activity of the Church. Jesus Christ becomes present with the power of the truth and the love that are expressed in him with unique unrepeatable fullness in spite of the shortness of his life on earth and the even greater shortness of his public activity.

Jesus Christ is the chief way for the Church. He himself is our way "to the Father's house"[88] and is the way to each man. On this way leading from Christ to man, on this way on which Christ unites himself with each man, nobody can halt the Church. This is an exigency of man's temporal welfare and of his eternal welfare. Out of regard for Christ and in view of the mystery that constitutes the Church's own life, the Church cannot remain insensible to whatever serves man's true welfare, any more than she can remain indifferent to what threatens it. In various passages in its documents the Second Vatican Council has expressed the Church's fundamental solicitude that life in "the world should conform more to man's surpassing dignity"[89] in all its aspects, so as to make that life "ever more human"[90]. This is the solicitude of Christ himself, the good Shepherd of all men. In the name of this solicitude, as we read in the Council's Pastoral Constitution, "the Church must in no way be confused with the political community, nor bound to any political system. She is at once a sign and a safeguard of the transcendence of the

---

[88] Cf. Jn 14:1ff.

[89] Vatican Council II: Pastoral Constitution on the Church in the Modern World *Gaudium et Spes*, 91: AAS 58 (1966) 1113.

[90] *Ibid.*, 38: 1. c., p. 1056.

human person".[91]

Accordingly, what is in question here is man in all his truth, in his full magnitude. We are not dealing with the "abstract" man, but the real, "concrete", "historical" man. We are dealing with "each" man, for each one is included in the mystery of the Redemption and with each one Christ has united himself for ever through this mystery. Every man comes into the world through being conceived in his mother's womb and being born of his mother, and precisely on account of the mystery of the Redemption is entrusted to the solicitude of the Church. Her solicitude is about the whole man and is focussed on him in an altogether special manner. The object of her care is man in his unique unrepeatable human reality, which keeps intact the image and likeness of God himself.[92] The Council points out this very fact when, speaking of that likeness, it recalls that "man is the only creature on earth that God willed for itself".[93] Man as "willed" by God, as "chosen" by him from eternity and called, destined for grace and glory—this is "each" man, "the most concrete" man, "the most real"; this is man in all the fullness of the mystery in which he has become a sharer in Jesus Christ, the mystery in which each one of the four thousand million human beings living on our planet has become a sharer from the moment he is conceived beneath the heart of his mother.

14. *For the Church all ways lead to man*

The Church cannot abandon man, for his "destiny", that is to say his election, calling, birth and death, salvation or perdition, is

---

[91] *Ibid.*, 76: 1. c., p. 1099.

[92] Cf. Gn 1:26.

[93] Vatican Council II: Pastoral Constitution on the Church in the Modern World *Gaudium et Spes*, 24: AAS 58 (1966) 1045.

so closely and unbreakably linked with Christ. We are speaking precisely of each man on this planet, this earth that the Creator gave to the first man, saying to the man and the women: "subdue it and have dominion".[94] Each man in all the unrepeatable reality of what he is and what he does, of his intellect and will, of his conscience and heart. Man who in his reality has, because he is a "person", a history of his life that is his own and, most important, a history of his soul that is his own. Man who, in keeping with the openness of his spirit within and also with the many diverse needs of his body and his existence in time, writes this personal history of his through numerous bonds, contacts, situations, and social structures linking him with other men, beginning to do so from the first moment of his existence on earth, from the moment of his conception and birth. Man in the full truth of his existence, of his personal being and also of his community and social being—in the sphere of his own family, in the sphere of society and very diverse contexts, in the sphere of his own nation or people (perhaps still only that of his clan or tribe), and in the sphere of the whole of mankind—this man is the primary route that the Church must travel in fulfilling her mission: he is the primary and fundamental way for the Church, the way traced out by Christ himself, the way that leads invariably through the mystery of the Incarnation and the Redemption.

It was precisely this man in all the truth of his life, in his conscience, in his continual inclination to sin and at the same time in his continual aspiration to truth, the good, the beautiful, justice and love that the Second Vatican Council had before its eyes when, in outlining his situation in the modern world, it always passed from the external elements of this situation

---

[94] Gn 1:28.

to the truth within humanity: "In man himself many elements wrestle with one another. Thus, on the one hand, as a creature he experiences his limitations in a multitude of ways. On the other, he feels himself to be boundless in his desires and summoned to a higher life. Pulled by manifold attractions, he is constantly forced to choose among them and to renounce some. Indeed, as a weak and sinful being, he often does what he would not, and fails to do what he would. Hence he suffers from internal divisions, and from these flow so many and such great discords in society".[95]

This man is the way for the Church—a way that, in a sense, is the basis of all the other ways that the Church must walk—because man—every man without any exception whatever—has been redeemed by Christ, and because with man—with each man without any exception whatever—Christ is in a way united, even when man is unaware of it: "Christ, who died and was raised up for all, provides man"–each man and every man— "with the light and the strength to measure up to his supreme calling".[96]

Since this man is the way for the Church, the way for her daily life and experience, for her mission and toil, the Church of today must be aware in an always new manner of man's "situation". That means that she must be aware of his possibilities, which keep returning to their proper bearings and thus revealing themselves. She must likewise be aware of the threats to man and of all that seems to oppose the endeavour "to make human life ever more human"[97] and make every element of this life

---

[95]   Vatican Council II: Pastoral Constitution on the Church in the Modern World *Gaudium et Spes*, 10: AAS 58 (1966) 1032.

[96]   *Ibid.*, 10: 1. c., p. 1033.

[97]   *Ibid.*, 38: 1. c., p. 1056; Pope Paul VI: Encyclical *Populorum Progressio*, 21: AAS 59 (1967) 267-268.

correspond to man's true dignity—in a word, she must be aware of *all that is opposed* to that process.

15. *What modern man is afraid of*

Accordingly, while keeping alive in our memory the picture that was so perspicaciously and authoritatively traced by the Second Vatican Council, we shall try once more to adapt it to the "signs of the times" and to the demands of the situation, which is continually changing and evolving in certain directions.

The man of today seems ever to be under threat from what he produces, that is to say from the result of the work of his hands and, even more so, of the work of his intellect and the tendencies of his will. All too soon, and often in an unforeseeable way, what this manifold activity of man yields is not only subjected to "alienation", in the sense that it is simply taken away from the person who produces it, but rather it turns against man himself, at least in part, through the indirect consequences of its effects returning on himself. It is or can be directed against him. This seems to make up the main chapter of the drama of present-day human existence in its broadest and universal dimension. Man therefore lives increasingly in fear. He is afraid that what he produces—not all of it, of course, or even most of it, but part of it and precisely that part that contains a special share of his genius and initiative—can radically turn against himself; he is afraid that it can become the means and instrument for an unimaginable self-destruction, compared with which all the cataclysms and catastrophes of history known to us seem to fade away. This gives rise to a question: Why is it that the power given to man from the beginning by which he was to subdue the earth[98] turns

---

[98] Cf. Gn 1:28.

against himself, producing an understandable state of disquiet, of conscious or unconscious fear and of menace, which in various ways is being communicated to the whole of the present-day human family and is manifesting itself under various aspects?

This state of menace for man from what he produces shows itself in various directions and various degrees of intensity. We seem to be increasingly aware of the fact that the exploitation of the earth, the planet on which we are living, demands rational and honest planning. At the same time, exploitation of the earth not only for industrial but also for military purposes and the uncontrolled development of technology outside the framework of a long-range authentically humanistic plan often bring with them a threat to man's natural environment, alienate him in his relations with nature and remove him from nature. Man often seems to see no other meaning in his natural environment than what serves for immediate use and consumption. Yet it was the Creator's will that man should communicate with nature as an intelligent and noble "master" and "guardian", and not as a heedless "exploiter" and "destroyer".

The development of technology and the development of contemporary civilization, which is marked by the ascendancy of technology, demand a proportional development of morals and ethics. For the present, this last development seems unfortunately to be always left behind. Accordingly, in spite of the marvel of this progress, in which it is difficult not to see also authentic signs of man's greatness, signs that in their creative seeds were revealed to us in the pages of the Book of Genesis, as early as where it describes man's creation,[99] this progress cannot fail to give rise to disquiet on many counts. The first reason

---

[99] Cf. Gn 1-2.

for disquiet concerns the essential and fundamental question: Does this progress, which has man for its author and promoter, make human life on earth "more human" in every aspect of that life? Does it make it more "worthy of man"? There can be no doubt that in various aspects it does. But the question keeps coming back with regard to what is most essential—whether in the context of this progress man, as man, is becoming truly better, that is to say more mature spiritually, more aware of the dignity of his humanity, more responsible, more open to others, especially the neediest and the weakest, and readier to give and to aid all.

This question must be put by Christians, precisely because Jesus Christ has made them so universally sensitive about the problem of man. The same question must be asked by all men, especially those belonging to the social groups that are dedicating themselves actively to development and progress today. As we observe and take part in these processes we cannot let ourselves be taken over merely by euphoria or be carried away by one-sided enthusiasm for our conquests, but we must all ask ourselves, with absolute honesty, objectivity and a sense of moral responsibility, the essential questions concerning man's situation today and in the future. Do all the conquests attained until now and those projected for the future for technology accord with man's moral and spiritual progress? In this context is man, as man, developing and progressing or is he regressing and being degraded in his humanity? In men and "in man's world", which in itself is a world of moral good and evil, does good prevail over evil? In men and among men is there a growth of social love, of respect for the rights of others—for every man, nation and people—or on the contrary is there an increase of various degrees of selfishness, exaggerated nationalism instead of authentic love of country, and also the propensity to dominate others beyond the limits of one's legitimate rights and merits and the propensity to exploit the whole of material progress and that in the technology of production for the exclusive purpose of dominating others or of favouring this or that imperialism?

These are the essential questions that the Church is bound to ask herself, since they are being asked with greater or less explicitness by the thousands of millions of people now living in the world. The subject of development and progress is on everybody's lips and appears in the columns of all the newspapers and other publications in all the languages of the modern world. Let us not forget however that this subject contains not only affirmations and certainties but also questions and points of anguished disquiet. The latter are no less important than the former. They fit in with the dialectical nature of human knowledge and even more with the fundamental need for solicitude by man for man, for his humanity, and for the future of people on earth. Inspired by eschatological faith, the Church considers an essential, unbreakably united element of her mission this solicitude for man, for his humanity, for the future of men on earth and therefore also for the course set for the whole of development and progress. She finds the principle of this solicitude in Jesus Christ himself, as the Gospels witness. This is why she wishes to make it grow continually through her relationship with Christ, reading man's situation in the modern world in accordance with the most important signs of our time.

16. *Progress or threat*

If therefore our time, the time of our generation, the time that is approaching the end of the second millennium of the Christian era, shows itself a time of great progress, it is also seen as a time of threat in many forms for man. The Church must speak of this threat to all people of good will and must always carry on a dialogue with them about it. Man's situation in the modern world seems indeed to be far removed from the objective demands of the moral order, from the requirements of justice, and even more of social love. We are dealing here only with that which found expression in the Creator's first message to man at the moment in which he was giving him the earth, to "subdue" it.[100] This first message was confirmed by Christ the Lord in the mystery of the Redemption. This is expressed by the Second Vatican Council in these beautiful chapters of its teaching that concern man's "kingship"; that is to say his call to share in the kingly function—the *munus regale* of Christ himself.[101] The essential meaning of this "kingship" and "dominion" of man over the visible world, which the Creator himself gave man for his task, consists in the priority of ethics over technology, in the primacy of the person over things, and in the superiority of spirit over matter.

This is why all phases of present-day progress must be followed attentively. Each stage of that progress must, so to speak, be x-rayed from this point of view. What is in question is the advancement of persons, not just the multiplying of things that people can use. It is a matter—as a contemporary philosopher has said and as the Council has stated—not so much of "having more" as of "being more".[102] Indeed there is already a real per-

---

[100] Gn 1:28; cf. Vatican Council II: Decree on the Social Communications Media *Inter Mirifica*, 6: AAS 56 (1964) 147; Pastoral Constitution on the Church in the Modern World *Gaudium et Spes*, 74, 78: AAS 58 (1966) 1095-1096, 1101-1102.

[101] Cf. Vatican Council II: Dogmatic Constitution on the Church *Lumen Gentium*, 10, 36: AAS 57 (1965) 14-15, 41-42.

[102] Cf. Vatican Council II: Pastoral Constitution on the Church in the Modern World *Gaudium et Spes*, 35: AAS 58 (1966) 1053; Pope Paul VI: *Address to*

ceptible danger that, while man's dominion over the world of things is making enormous advances, he should lose the essential threads of his dominion and in various ways let his humanity be subjected to the world and become himself something subject to manipulation in many ways—even if the manipulation is often not perceptible directly—through the whole of the organization of community life, through the production system and through pressure from the means of social communication. Man cannot relinquish himself or the place in the visible world that belongs to him; he cannot become the slave of things, the slave of economic systems, the slave of production, the slave of his own products. A civilization purely materialistic in outline condemns man to such slavery, even if at times, no doubt, this occurs contrary to the intentions and the very premises of its pioneers. The present solicitude for man certainly has at its root this problem. It is not a matter here merely of giving an abstract answer to the question: Who is man? It is a matter of the whole of the dynamism of life and civilization. It is a matter of the meaningfulness of the various initiatives of everyday life and also of the premises for many civilization programmes, political programmes, eco nomic ones, social ones, state ones, and many others.

If we make bold to describe man's situation in the modern world as far removed from the objective demands of the moral order, from the exigencies of justice, and still more from social love, we do so because this is confirmed by the well-known facts and comparisons that have already on various occasions found an echo in the pages of statements by the Popes, the Council and the Synod.[103] Man's situation today is certainly not uniform

---

Diplomatic Corps, January 7, 1965: AAS 57 (1965) 232; Encyclical *Populorum Progressio,* 14: AAS 59 (1967) 264.

[103] Cf. Pope Pius XII: *Radio Message on the Fiftieth Anniversary of Leo XIII's En-*

but marked with numerous differences. These differences have causes in history, but they also have strong ethical effects. Indeed everyone is familiar with the picture of the consumer civilization, which consists in a certain surplus of goods necessary for man and for entire societies—and we are dealing precisely with the rich highly developed societies—while the remaining societies— at least broad sectors of them—are suffering from hunger, with many people dying each day of starvation and malnutrition. Hand in hand go a certain abuse of freedom by one group—an abuse linked precisely with a consumer attitude uncontrolled by

---

cyclical *"Rerum Novarum,"* June 1, 1941: AAS 33 (1941) 195-205; *Christmas Radio Message*, December 24, 1941: AAS 34 (1942) 10-21; *Christmas Radio Message*, December 24, 1942: AAS 35 (1943) 9-24; *Christmas Radio Message*, December 24, 1943: AAS 36 (1944) 11-24; *Christmas Radio Message*, December 24, 1944: AAS 37 (1945) 10-23; *Address to the Cardinals*, December 24, 1945: AAS 38 (1946) 15-25; *Address to the Cardinals*, December 24, 1946: AAS 39 (1947) 7-17; *Christmas Radio Message*, December 24, 1947: AAS 40 (1948) 8-16; Pope John XXIII: Encyclical *Mater et Magistra:* AAS 53 (1961) 401-464; Encyclical *Pacem in Terris:* AAS 55 (1963) 257-304; Pope Paul VI: Encyclical *Ecclesiam Suam:* AAS 56 (1964) 609-659; *Address to the General Assembly of the United Nations*, October 4, 1965: AAS 57 (1965) 877-885; Encyclical *Populorum Progressio:* AAS 59 (1967) 257-299; *Address to the Campesinos of Colombia*, August 23, 1968: RRS 60 (1968) 619-623; *Speech to the General Assembly of the Latin-American Episcopate*, August 24, 1968: AAS 60 (1968) 639-649; *Speech to the Conference of FAO*, November 16, 1970: AAS 62 (1970) 830-838; Apostolic Letter *Octogesima Adveniens:* AAS 63 (1971) 401-441; *Address to the Cardinals*, June 23, 1972: AAS 64 (1972) 496-505; Pope Paul VI: *Address to the Third General Conference of the Latin-American Episcopate*, January 28, 1979: AAS 71 (1979) 187ff.; *Address to the Indians at Cuilipan*, January 29, 1979: 1. c., pp. 207ff.; *Address to the Guadalajara Workers*, January 30, 1979: 1. c., pp. 221ff.; *Address to the Monterrey Workers*, January 31, 1979: 1. c., pp. 240-242; Vatican Council II: Declaration on Religious Freedom *Dignitatis Humanae:* AAS 58 (1966) 929-941; Pastoral Constitution on the Church in the Modern World *Gaudium et Spes:* AAS 58 (1966) 1025-1115; Documenta Synodi Episcoporum: *De iustitia in mundo:* AAS 63 (1971) 923-941.

ethics—and a limitation by it of the freedom of the others, that is to say those suffering marked shortages and being driven to conditions of even worse misery and destitution.

This pattern, which is familiar to all, and the contrast referred to, in the documents giving their teaching, by the Popes of this century, most recently by John XXIII and by Paul VI,[104] represent, as it were, the gigantic development of the parable in the Bible of the rich banqueter and the poor man Lazarus.[105] So widespread is the phenomenon that it brings into question the financial, monetary, production and commercial mechanisms that, resting on various political pressures, support the world economy. These are proving incapable either of remedying the unjust social situations inherited from the past or of dealing with the urgent challenges and ethical demands of the present. By submitting man to tensions created by himself, dilapidating at an accelerated pace material and energy resources, and compromising the geophysical environment, these structures unceasingly make the areas of misery spread, accompanied by anguish, frustration and bitterness.[106]

We have before us here a great drama that can leave nobody indifferent. The person who, on the one hand, is trying to draw the maximum profit and, on the other hand, is paying the price in damage and injury is always man. The drama is made still worse by the presence close at hand of the privileged social classes and

---

[104] Cf. Pope John XXIII: Encyclical *Mater et Magistra:* AAS 53 (1961) 418ff.; Encyclical *Pacem in Terris:* AAS 55 (1963) 289ff.; Pope Paul VI, Encyclical *Populorum Progressio* AAS 59 (1967) 257-299.

[105] Cf. Lk 16:19-31.

[106] Cf. Pope John Paul II: *Homily at Santo Domingo,* January 25, 1979, 3: AAS 71 (1979) 157ff.; *Address to Indians and Campesinos at Oaxaca,* January 30, 1979, 2: 1. c., pp. 207ff.; *Address to Monterrey Workers,* January 31, 1979, 4: 1. c., p. 242.

of the rich countries, which accumulate goods to an excessive degree and the misuse of whose riches very often becomes the cause of various ills. Add to this the fever of inflation and the plague of unemployment—these are further symptoms of the moral disorder that is being noticed in the world situation and therefore requires daring creative resolves in keeping with man's authentic dignity.[107]

Such a task is not an impossible one. The principle of solidarity, in a wide sense, must inspire the effective search for appropriate institutions and mechanisms, whether in the sector of trade, where the laws of healthy competition must be allowed to lead the way, or on the level of a wider and more immediate redistribution of riches and of control over them, in order that the economically developing peoples may be able not only to satisfy their essential needs but also to advance gradually and effectively.

This difficult road of the indispensable transformation of the structures of economic life is one on which it will not be easy to go forward without the intervention of a true conversion of mind, will and heart. The task requires resolute commitment by individuals and peoples that are free and linked in solidarity. All too often freedom is confused with the instinct for individual or collective interest or with the instinct for combat and domination, whatever be the ideological colours with which they are covered. Obviously these instincts exist and are operative, but no truly human economy will be possible unless they are taken up, directed and dominated by the deepest powers in man, which decide the true culture of peoples. These are the very sources for the effort which will express man's true freedom and

---

[107] Cf. Pope Paul VI, Apostolic Letter *Octogesima Adveniens*, 42: AAS 63 (1971) 431.

which will be capable of ensuring it in the economic field also. Economic development, with every factor in its adequate functioning, must be constantly programmed and realized within a perspective of universal joint development of each individual and people, as was convincingly recalled by my Predecessor Paul VI in *Populorum Progressio*. Otherwise, the category of "economic progress" becomes in isolation a superior category subordinating the whole of human existence to its partial demands, suffocating man, breaking up society, and ending by entangling itself in its own tensions and excesses.

It is possible to undertake this duty. This is testified by the certain facts and the results, which it would be difficult to mention more analytically here. However, one thing is certain: at the basis of this gigantic sector it is necessary to establish, accept and deepen the sense of moral responsibility, which man must undertake. Again and always man.

This responsibility becomes especially evident for us Christians when we recall—and we should always recall it—the scene of the last judgment according to the words of Christ related in Matthew's Gospel.[108]

This eschatological scene must always be "applied" to man's history; it must always be made the "measure" for human acts as an essential outline for an examination of conscience by each and every one: "I was hungry and you gave me no food . . . naked and you did not clothe me . . . in prison and you did not visit me".[109] These words become charged with even stronger warning, when we think that, instead of bread and cultural aid, the new States and nations awakening to independent life are being offered, sometimes in abundance, modern weapons and

---

[108] Cf. Mt 25:31-46.
[109] Mt 25:42, 43.

means of destruction placed at the service of armed conflicts and wars that are not so much a requirement for defending their just rights and their sovereignty but rather a form of chauvinism, imperialism, and neocolonialism of one kind or another. We all know well that the areas of misery and hunger on our globe could have been made fertile in a short time, if the gigantic investments for armaments at the service of war and destruction had been changed into investments for food at the service of life.

This consideration will perhaps remain in part an "abstract" one. It will perhaps offer both "sides" an occasion for mutual accusation, each forgetting its own faults. It will perhaps provoke new accusations against the Church. The Church, however, which has no weapons at her disposal apart from those of the spirit, of the word and of love, cannot renounce her proclamation of "the word . . . in season and out of season".[110] For this reason she does not cease to implore each side of the two and to beg everybody in the name of God and in the name of man: Do not kill! Do not prepare destruction and extermination for men! Think of your brothers and sisters who are suffering hunger and misery! Respect each one's dignity and freedom!

17. *Human rights: "letter" or "spirit"*

This century has so far been a century of great calamities for man, of great devastations, not only material ones but also moral ones, indeed perhaps above all moral ones. Admittedly it is not easy to compare one age or one century with another under this aspect, since that depends also on changing historical standards. Nevertheless, without applying these comparisons, one still cannot fail to see that this century has so far been one in which people

---

[110] 2 Tm 4:2.

have provided many injustices and sufferings for themselves. Has this process been decisively curbed? In any case, we cannot fail to recall at this point, with esteem and profound hope for the future, the magnificent effort made to give life to the United Nations Organization, an effort conducive to the definition and establishment of man's objective and inviolable rights, with the member States obliging each other to observe them rigorously. This commitment has been accepted and ratified by almost all present-day States, and this should constitute a guarantee that human rights will become throughout the world a fundamental principle of work for man's welfare.

There is no need for the Church to confirm how closely this problem is linked with her mission in the modern world. Indeed it is at the very basis of social and international peace, as has been declared by John XXIII, the Second Vatican Council, and later Paul VI, in detailed documents. After all, peace comes down to respect for man's inviolable rights—*Opus iustitiae pax*—while war springs from the violation of these rights and brings with it still graver violations of them. If human rights are violated in time of peace, this is particularly painful and from the point of view of progress it represents an incomprehensible manifestation of activity directed against man, which can in no way be reconciled with any programme that describes itself as "humanistic". And what social, economic, political or cultural programme could renounce this description? We are firmly convinced that there is no programme in today's world in which man is not invariably brought to the fore, even when the platforms of the programmes are made up of conflicting ideologies concerning the way of conceiving the world.

If, in spite of these premises, human rights are being violated in various ways, if in practice we see before us concentration camps, violence, torture, terrorism, and discrimination in many forms, this must then be the consequence of the other premises, undermining and often almost annihilating the effectiveness of the humanistic premises of these modern programmes and systems. This necessarily imposes the duty to submit these programmes to continual revision from the point of view of the objective and inviolable rights of man.

The Declaration of Human Rights linked with the setting up of the United Nations Organization certainly had as its aim not only to depart from the horrible experiences of the last world war but also to create the basis for continual revision of programmes, systems and regimes precisely from this single fundamental point of view, namely the welfare of man-or, let us say, of the person in the community-which must, as a fundamental factor in the common good, constitute the essential criterion for all programmes, systems and regimes. If the opposite happens, human life is, even in time of peace, condemned to various sufferings and, along with these sufferings, there is a development of various forms of domination, totalitarianism, neocolonialism and imperialism, which are a threat also to the harmonious living together of the nations. Indeed, it is a significant fact, repeatedly confirmed by the experiences of history, that violation of the rights of man goes hand in hand with violation of the rights of the nation, with which man is united by organic links as with a larger family.

Already in the first half of this century, when various State totalitarianisms were developing, which, as is well known, led to the horrible catastrophe of war, the Church clearly outlined her position with regard to these regimes that to all appearances were acting for a higher good, namely the good of the State, while history was to show instead that the good in question was only that of a certain party, which had been identified with the

State.[111] In reality, those regimes had restricted the rights of the citizens, denying them recognition precisely of those inviolable human rights that have reached formulation on the international level in the middle of our century. While sharing the joy of all people of good will, of all people who truly love justice and peace, at this conquest, the Church, aware that the "letter" on its own can kill, while only "the spirit gives life",[112] must continually ask, together with these people of good will, whether the Declaration of Human Rights and the acceptance of their "letter" mean everywhere also the actualization of their "spirit". Indeed, well founded fears arise that very often we are still far from this actualization and that at times the spirit of social and public life is painfully opposed to the declared "letter" of human rights. This state of things, which is burdensome for the societies concerned, would place special responsibility towards these societies and the history of man on those contributing to its establishment.

The essential sense of the State, as a political community, consists in that the society and people composing it are master and sovereign of their own destiny. This sense remains unrealized if, instead of the exercise of power with the moral participation of the society or people, what we see is the imposition of power by a certain group upon all the other members of the society. This is essential in the present age, with its enormous increase in people's social awareness and the accompanying need for the citizens to have a right share in the political life of the commu-

---

[111] Pope Pius XI: Encyclical *Quadragesimo Anno:* AAS 23 (1931) 213; Encyclical *Non Abbiamo Bisogno:* AAS 23 (1931) 285-312; Encyclical *Divini Redemptoris:* AAS 29 (1937) 65-106; Encyclical *Mit brennender Sorge:* AAS 29 (1937) 145-147; Pope Pius XII: Encyclical *Summi Pontificates:* AAS 31 (1939) 413-453.

[112] Cf. 2 Cor 3:6.

nity, while taking account of the real conditions of each people and the necessary vigour of public authority.[113] These therefore are questions of primary importance from the point of view of the progress of man himself and the overall development of his humanity.

The Church has always taught the duty to act for the common good and, in so doing, has likewise educated good citizens for each State. Furthermore, she has always taught that the fundamental duty of power is solicitude for the common good of society; this is what gives power its fundamental rights. Precisely in the name of these premises of the objective ethical order, the rights of power can only be understood on the basis of respect for the objective and inviolable rights of man. The common good that authority in the State serves is brought to full realization only when all the citizens are sure of their rights. The lack of this leads to the dissolution of society, opposition by citizens to authority, or a situation of oppression, intimidation, violence, and terrorism, of which many examples have been provided by the totalitarianisms of this century. Thus the principle of human rights is of profound concern to the area of social justice and is the measure by which it can be tested in the life of political bodies.

These rights are rightly reckoned to include the right to religious freedom together with the right to freedom of conscience. The Second Vatican Council considered especially necessary the preparation of a fairly long declaration on this subject. This is the document called *Dignitatis Humanae*,[114] in which is expressed not only the theological concept of the question but

---

[113] Cf. Vatican Council II: Pastoral Constitution on the Church in the Modern World *Gaudium et Spes*, 31: AAS 58 (1966) 1050.

[114] Cf. AAS 58 (1966) 929-946.

also the concept reached from the point of view of natural law, that is to say from the "purely human" position, on the basis of the premises given by man's own experience, his reason and his sense of human dignity. Certainly the curtailment of the religious freedom of individuals and communities is not only a painful experience but it is above all an attack on man's very dignity, independently of the religion professed or of the concept of the world which these individuals and communities have. The curtailment and violation of religious freedom are in contrast with man's dignity and his objective rights. The Council document mentioned above states clearly enough what that curtailment or violation of religious freedom is. In this case we are undoubtedly confronted with a radical injustice with regard to what is particularly deep within man, what is authentically human. Indeed, even the phenomenon of unbelief, a-religiousness and atheism, as a human phenomenon, is understood only in relation to the phenomenon of religion and faith. It is therefore difficult, even from a "purely human" point of view, to accept a position that gives only atheism the right of citizenship in public and social life, while believers are, as though by principle, barely tolerated or are treated as second-class citizens or are even-and this has already happened-entirely deprived of the rights of citizenship.

Even if briefly, this subject must also be dealt with, because it too enters into the complex of man's situations in the present-day world and because it too gives evidence of the degree to which this situation is overburdened by prejudices and injustices of various kinds. If we refrain from entering into details in this field in which we would have a special right and duty to do so, it is above all because, together with all those who are suffering the torments of discrimination and persecution for the name of God, we are guided by faith in the redeeming power of the

Cross of Christ. However, because of my office, I appeal in the name of all believers throughout the world to those on whom the organization of social and public life in some way depends, earnestly requesting them to respect the rights of religion and of the Church's activity. No privilege is asked for, but only respect for an elementary right. Actuation of this right is one of the fundamental tests of man's authentic progress in any regime, in any society, system or milieu.

IV.   The Church's Mission and Man's Destiny

18.   *The Church as concerned for man's vocation in Christ*

This necessarily brief look at man's situation in the modern world makes us direct our thoughts and our hearts to Jesus Christ, and to the mystery of the Redemption, in which the question of man is inscribed with a special vigour of truth and love. If Christ "united himself with each man",[115] the Church lives more profoundly her own nature and mission by penetrating into the depths of this mystery and into its rich universal language. It was not without reason that the Apostle speaks of Christ's Body, the Church.[116] If this Mystical Body of Christ is God's People-as the Second Vatican Council was to say later on the basis of the whole of the Biblical and patristic tradition-his means that in it each man receives within himself that breath of life that comes from Christ. In this way, turning to man and his real problems, his hopes and sufferings, his achievements and falls-this too also makes the

---

[115] Vatican Council II: Pastoral Constitution on the Church in the Modern World *Gaudium et Spes*, 22: AAS 58 (1966) 1042.

[116] Cf. 1 Cor 6:15; 11:3; 12:12-13; Eph 1:22-23; 2:15-16; 4:4-6; 5:30; Col 1:18; 3:15; Rom 12:4-5; Gal 3:28.

Church as a body, an organism, a social unit perceive the same divine influences, the light and strength of the Spirit that come from the crucified and risen Christ, and it is for this very reason that she lives her life. The Church has only one life: that which is given her by her Spouse and Lord. Indeed, precisely because Christ united himself with her in his mystery of Redemption, the Church must be strongly united with each man.

This union of Christ with man is in itself a mystery. From the mystery is born "the new man", called to become a partaker of God's life,[117] and newly created in Christ for the fullness of grace and truth.[118] Christ's union with man is power and the source of power, as Saint John stated so incisively in the prologue of his Gospel: "(The Word) gave power to become children of God".[119] Man is transformed inwardly by this power as the source of a new life that does not disappear and pass away but lasts to eternal life.[120] This life, which the Father has promised and offered to each man in Jesus Christ, his eternal and only Son, who, "when the time had fully come",[121] became incarnate and was born of the Virgin Mary, is the final fulfilment of man's vocation. It is in a way the fulfilment of the "destiny" that God has prepared for him from eternity. This "divine destiny" is advancing, in spite of all the enigmas, the unsolved riddles, the twists and turns of "human destiny" in the world of time. Indeed, while all this, in spite of all the riches of life in time, necessarily and inevitably leads to the frontier of death and the goal of the destruction of the human body, beyond that goal we see Christ. "I am the

---

[117] 2 Pt 1:4.

[118] Cf. Eph 2:10; Jn 1:14, 16.

[119] Jn 1:12.

[120] Cf. Jn 4:14.

[121] Gal 4:4.

resurrection and the life, he who believes in me . . . shall never die".[122] In Jesus Christ, who was crucified and laid in the tomb and then rose again, "our hope of resurrection dawned . . . the bright promise of immortality",[123] on the way to which man, through the death of the body, shares with the whole of visible creation the necessity to which matter is subject. We intend and are trying to fathom ever more deeply the language of the truth that man's Redeemer enshrined in the phrase "It is the spirit that gives life, the flesh is of no avail".[124] In spite of appearances, these words express the highest affirmation of man-the affirmation of the body given life by the Spirit.

The Church lives these realities, she lives by this truth about man, which enables him to go beyond the bounds of temporariness and at the same time to think with particular love and solicitude of everything within the dimensions of this temporariness that affect man's life and the life of the human spirit, in which is expressed that never-ending restlessness referred to in the words of Saint Augustine: "You made us for yourself, Lord, and our heart is restless until it rests in you".[125] In this creative restlessness beats and pulsates what is most deeply human-the search for truth, the insatiable need for the good, hunger for freedom, nostalgia for the beautiful, and the voice of conscience. Seeking to see man as it were with "the eyes of Christ himself", the Church becomes more and more aware that she is the guardian of a great treasure, which she may not waste but must continually increase. Indeed, the Lord Jesus said: "He who

---

[122] Jn 11:25-26.
[123] Preface of Christian Death, I.
[124] Jn 6:63.
[125] *Confessio*, I, 1: CSEL 33, p. 1.

does not gather with me scatters".[126] This treasure of humanity enriched by the inexpressible mystery of divine filiation[127] and by the grace of "adoption as sons"[128] in the Only Son of God, through whom we call God "Abba, Father",[129] is also a powerful force unifying the Church above all inwardly and giving meaning to all her activity. Through this force the Church is united with the Spirit of Christ, that Holy Spirit promised and continually communicated by the Redeemer and whose descent, which was revealed on the day of Pentecost, endures for ever. Thus the powers of the Spirit,[130] the gifts of the Spirit,[131] and the fruits of the Holy Spirit[132] are revealed in men. The present-day Church seems to repeat with ever greater fervour and with holy insistence: "Come, Holy Spirit!". Come! Come! "Heal our wounds, our strength renew; On our dryness pour your dew; Wash the stains of guilt away; Bend the stubborn heart and will; Melt the frozen, warm the chill; Guide the steps that go astray".[133]

This appeal to the Spirit, intended precisely to obtain the Spirit, is the answer to all the "materialisms" of our age. It is these materialisms that give birth to so many forms of insatiability in the human heart. This appeal is making itself heard on various sides and seems to be bearing fruit also in different ways. Can it be said that the Church is not alone in making this appeal? Yes it can, because the "need" for what is spiritual is expressed also by people who are outside the visible confines

---

[126] Mt 12:30.

[127] Cf. Jn 1:12.

[128] Gal 4:5.

[129] Gal 4: 6; Rom 8:15.

[130] Cf. Rom 15:13; 1 Cor 1:24.

[131] Cf. Is 11:2-3; Acts 2:38.

[132] Cf. Gal 5:22-23.

[133] Sequence for Pentecost.

of the Church.[134] Is not this confirmed by the truth concerning the Church that the recent Council so acutely emphasized at the point in the Dogmatic Constitution *Lumen Gentium* where it teaches that the Church is a "sacrament or sign and means of intimate union with God, and of the unity of all mankind?".[135] This invocation addressed to the Spirit to obtain the Spirit is really a constant self-insertion into the full magnitude of the mystery of the Redemption, in which Christ, united with the Father and with each man, continually communicates to us the Spirit who places within us the sentiments of the Son and directs us towards the Father.[136] This is why the Church of our time-a time particularly hungry for the Spirit, because it is hungry for justice, peace, love, goodness, fortitude, responsibility, and human dignity-must concentrate and gather around that Mystery, finding in it the light and the strength that are indispensable for her mission. For if, as was already said, man is the way for the Church's daily life, the Church must be always aware of the dignity of the divine adoption received by man in Christ through the grace of the Holy Spirit[137] and of his destination to grace and glory.[138] By reflecting ever anew on all this, and by accepting it with a faith that is more and more aware and a love that is more and more firm, the Church also makes herself better fitted for the service to man to which Christ the Lord calls her when he says: "The Son of man came not to be served but to serve".[139] The Church performs this ministry by sharing in the "triple office"

---

[134] Cf. Vatican Council II: Dogmatic Constitution on the Church *Lumen Gentium*, 16: AAS 57 (1965) 20.

[135] *Ibid.*, 1: 1. c., p. 5.

[136] Cf. Rom 8:15; Gal 4:6.

[137] Cf. Rom 8:15.

[138] Cf. Rom 8:30.

[139] Mt 20:28.

belonging to her Master and Redeemer. This teaching, with its Biblical foundation, was brought fully to the fore by the Second Vatican Council, to the great advantage of the Church's life. For when we become aware that we share in Christ's triple mission, his triple office as priest, as prophet and as king,[140] we also become more aware of what must receive service from the whole of the Church as the society and community of the People of God on earth, and we likewise understand how each one of us must share in this mission and service.

19. *The Church as responsible for truth*

In the light of the sacred teaching of the Second Vatican Council, the Church thus appears before us as the social subject of responsibility for divine truth. With deep emotion we hear Christ himself saying: "The word which you hear is not mine but the Father's who sent me".[141] In this affirmation by our Master do we not notice responsibility for the revealed truth, which is the "property" of God himself, since even he, "the only Son", who lives "in the bosom of the Father",[142] when transmitting that truth as a prophet and teacher, feels the need to stress that he is acting in full fidelity to its divine source? The same fidelity must be a constitutive quality of the Church's faith, both when she is teaching it and when she is professing it. Faith as a specific supernatural virtue infused into the human spirit makes us sharers in knowledge of God as a response to his revealed word. Therefore it is required, when the Church professes and teaches

---

[140] Vatican Council II: Dogmatic Constitution on the Church *Lumen Gentium*, 31-36: AAS 57 (1965) 37-42.

[141] Jn 14:24.

[142] Jn 1:18.

the faith, that she should adhere strictly to divine truth,[143] and should translate it into living attitudes of "obedience in harmony with reason".[144] Christ himself, concerned for this fidelity to divine truth, promised the Church the special assistance of the Spirit of truth, gave the gift of infallibility[145] to those whom he entrusted with the mandate of transmitting and teaching that truth[146]—as has besides been clearly defined by the First Vatican Council[147] and has then been repeated by the Second Vatican Council[148]—and he furthermore endowed the whole of the People of God with a special sense of the faith.[149]

Consequently, we have become sharers in this mission of the prophet Christ, and in virtue of that mission we together with him are serving divine truth in the Church. Being responsible for that truth also means loving it and seeking the most exact understanding of it, in order to bring it closer to ourselves and others in all its saving power, its splendour and its profundity joined with simplicity. This love and this aspiration to understand the truth must go hand in hand, as is confirmed by the histories of the saints in the Church. These received most brightly the

---

[143] Cf. Vatican Council II: Dogmatic Constitution on Divine Revelation *Dei Verbum*, 5, 10, 21: AAS 58 (1966) 819, 822, 827-828.

[144] Cf. Vatican Council I: Dogmatic Constitution on the Catholic Faith *Dei Filius*, Chap. 3: *Conciliorum Oecumenicorum Decreta*, Ed. Istituto per le Scienze Religiose, Bologna 1973 3, p. 807.

[145] Cf. Vatican Council I: First Dogmatic Constitution on the Church of Christ Pastor Aeternus: 1. c., pp. 811-816; Vatican Council II: Dogmatic Constitution *Lumen Gentium*, 25: AAS 57 (1965) pp. 30-31.

[146] Cf. Mt 28:19.

[147] Cf. Vatican Council I: First Dogmatic Constitution on the Church of Christ *Pastor Aeternus:* 1. c., pp. 811-816.

[148] Cf. Vatican Council II: Dogmatic Constitution on the Church *Lumen Gentium*, 18-27: AAS 57 (1965) 21-23.

[149] Cf. *Ibid.*, 12, 35: 1. c., pp. 16-17, 40-41.

authentic light that illuminates divine truth and brings close God's very reality, because they approached this truth with veneration and love-love in the first place for Christ, the living Word of divine truth, and then love for his human expression in the Gospel, tradition and theology. Today we still need above all that understanding and interpretation of God's Word; we need that theology. Theology has always had and continues to have great importance for the Church, the People of God, to be able to share creatively and fruitfully in Christ's mission as prophet. Therefore, when theologians, as servants of divine truth, dedicate their studies and labours to ever deeper understanding of that truth, they can never lose sight of the meaning of their service in the Church, which is enshrined in the concept *intellectus fidei*. This concept has, so to speak, a two-way function, in line with Saint Augustine's expression: *intellege, utcredas-crede, ut intellegas*,[150] and it functions correctly when they seek to serve the Magisterium, which in the Church is entrusted to the Bishops joined by the bond of hierarchical communion with Peter's Successor, when they place themselves at the service of their solicitude in teaching and giving pastoral care, and when they place themselves at the service of the apostolic commitments of the whole of the People of God.

As in preceding ages, and perhaps more than in preceding ages, theologians and all men of learning in the Church are today called to unite faith with learning and wisdom, in order to help them to combine with each other, as we read in the prayer in the liturgy of the memorial of Saint Albert, Doctor of the Church. This task has grown enormously today because of the advance of human learning, its methodology, and the achievements in

---

[150] Cf. St. Augustine: *Sermo* 43, 79: PL 38, 257-258.

knowledge of the world and of man. This concerns both the exact sciences and the human sciences, as well as philosophy, which, as the Second Vatican Council recalled, is closely linked with theology.[151]

In this field of human knowledge, which is continually being broadened and yet differentiated, faith too must be investigated deeply, manifesting the magnitude of revealed mystery and tending towards an understanding of truth, which has in God its one supreme source. If it is permissible and even desirable that the enormous work to be done in this direction should take into consideration a certain pluralism of methodology, the work cannot however depart from the fundamental unity in the teaching of Faith and Morals which is that work's end. Accordingly, close collaboration by theology with the Magisterium is indispensable. Every theologian must be particularly aware of what Christ himself stated when he said: "The word which you hear is not mine but the Father's who sent me".[152] Nobody, therefore, can make of theology as it were a simple collection of his own personal ideas, but everybody must be aware of being in close union with the mission of teaching truth for which the Church is responsible.

The sharing in the prophetic office of Christ himself shapes the life of the whole of the Church in her fundamental dimension. A particular share in this office belongs to the Pastors of the Church, who teach and continually and in various ways proclaim and transmit the doctrine concerning the Christian faith and morals. This teaching, both in its missionary and its ordinary aspect, helps to assemble the People of God around Christ, pre-

---

[151] Cf. Vatican Council II: Pastoral Constitution on the Church in the Modern World *Gaudium et Spes*, 44, 57, 59, 62: AAS 58 (1966) 1064f., 1077ff., 1079f., 1082ff.; Decree on Priestly Training *Optatam Totius*, 15: AAS 58 (1966) 722.

[152] Jn 14:24.

pares for participation in the Eucharist and points out the ways for sacramental life. In 1977 the Synod of the Bishops dedicated special attention to catechesis in the modern world, and the mature results of its deliberations, experiences and suggestions will shortly find expression—in keeping with the proposal made by the participants in the Synod—in a special papal document. Catechesis certainly constitutes a permanent and also fundamental form of activity by the Church, one in which her prophetic charism is manifested: witnessing and teaching go hand in hand. And although here we are speaking in the first place of priests, it is however impossible not to mention also the great number of men and women religious dedicating themselves to catechetical activity for love of the divine Master. Finally, it would be difficult not to mention the many lay people who find expression in this activity for their faith and their apostolic responsibility.

Furthermore, increasing care must be taken that the various forms of catechesis and its various fields—beginning with the fundamental field, family catechesis, that is the catechesis by parents of their children—should give evidence of the universal sharing by the whole of the People of God in the prophetic office of Christ himself. Linked with this fact, the Church's responsibility for divine truth must be increasingly shared in various ways by all. What shall we say at this point with regard to the specialists in the various disciplines, those who represent the natural sciences and letters, doctors, jurists, artists and technicians, teachers at various levels and with different specializations? As members of the People of God, they all have their own part to play in Christ's prophetic mission and service of divine truth, among other ways by an honest attitude towards truth, whatever field it may belong to, while educating others in truth and teaching them to mature in love and justice. Thus, a sense of responsibility for truth is one of the fundamental points of encounter between the Church and each man and also one of the fundamental demands determining man's vocation in the community of the Church. The present-day Church, guided by a sense of responsibility for truth, must persevere in fidelity to her own nature, which involves the prophetic mission that comes from Christ himself: "As the Father has sent me, even so I send you . . . Receive the Holy Spirit".[153]

20. *Eucharist and Penance*

In the mystery of the Redemption, that is to say in Jesus Christ's saving work, the Church not only shares in the Gospel of her Master through fidelity to the word and service of truth, but she also shares, through a submission filled with hope and love, in the power of his redeeming action expressed and enshrined by him in a sacramental form, especially in the Eucharist.[154] The Eucharist is the centre and summit of the whole of sacramental life, through which each Christian receives the saving power of the Redemption, beginning with the mystery of Baptism, in which we are buried into the death of Christ, in order to become sharers in his Resurrection,[155] as the Apostle teaches. In the light of this teaching, we see still more clearly the reason why the entire sacramental life of the Church and of each Christian reaches its summit and fullness in the Eucharist. For by Christ's will there is in this Sacrament a continual renewing of the mystery of the Sacrifice of himself that Christ offered to the Father on the altar of the Cross, a Sacrifice that the Father accepted, giving, in

---

[153] Jn 20:21-22.

[154] Cf. Vatican Council II: Constitution on the Sacred Liturgy *Sacrosanctum Concilium*, 10: AAS 56 (1964) 102.

[155] Cf. Rom 6:3-5.

return for this total self-giving by his Son, who "became obedient unto death",[156] his own paternal gift, that is to say the grant of new immortal life in the resurrection, since the Father is the first source and the giver of life from the beginning. That new life, which involves the bodily glorification of the crucified Christ, became an efficacious sign of the new gift granted to humanity, the gift that is the Holy Spirit, through whom the divine life that the Father has in himself and gives to his Son[157] is communicated to all men who are united with Christ.

The Eucharist is the most perfect Sacrament of this union. By celebrating and also partaking of the Eucharist we unite ourselves with Christ on earth and in heaven who intercedes for us with the Father[158] but we always do so through the redeeming act of his Sacrifice, through which he has redeemed us, so that we have been "bought with a price".[159] The "price" of our redemption is likewise a further proof of the value that God himself sets on man and of our dignity in Christ. For by becoming "children of God",[160] adopted sons,[161] we also become in his likeness "a kingdom and priests" and obtain "a royal priesthood",[162] that is to say we share in that unique and irreversible restoration of man and the world to the Father that was carried out once for all by him, who is both the eternal Son[163] and also true Man. The Eucharist is the Sacrament in which our new being is most

---

[156] Phil 2:8.

[157] Cf. Jn 5:26; 1 Jn 5:11.

[158] Heb 9:24; 1 Jn 2:1.

[159] 1 Cor 6:20.

[160] Jn 1:12.

[161] Cf. Rom 8:23.

[162] Rv 5:10; 1 Pt 2:9.

[163] Cf. Jn 1:1-4, 18; Mt 3:17; 11:27; 17:5; Mk 1:11; Lk 1:32, 35; 3:22; Rom 1:4; 2 Cor 1:19; 1 Jn 5:5, 20; 2 Pt 1:17; Heb 1:2.

completely expressed and in which Christ himself unceasingly and in an ever new manner "bears witness" in the Holy Spirit to our spirit[164] that each of us, as a sharer in the mystery of the Redemption, has access to the fruits of the filial reconciliation with God[165] that he himself actuated and continually actuates among us by means of the Church's ministry.

It is an essential truth, not only of doctrine but also of life, that the Eucharist builds the Church,[166] building it as the authentic community of the People of God, as the assembly of the faithful, bearing the same mark of unity that was shared by the Apostles and the first disciples of the Lord. The Eucharist builds ever anew this community and unity, ever building and regenerating it on the basis of the Sacrifice of Christ, since it commemorates his death on the Cross,[167] the price by which he redeemed us. Accordingly, in the Eucharist we touch in a way the very mystery of the Body and Blood of the Lord, as is attested by the very words used at its institution, the words that, because of that institution, have become the words with which those called to this ministry in the Church un ceasingly celebrate the Eucharist.

The Church lives by the Eucharist, by the fullness of this Sacrament, the stupendous content and meaning of which have often been expressed in the Church's Magisterium from the most distant times down to our own days.[168] However, we can say with certainty that, although this teaching is sustained by the

---

[164] Cf. 1 Jn 5:5-11.

[165] Cf. Rom 5:10, 11; 2 Cor 5:18-19; Col 1:20, 22.

[166] Cf. Vatican Council II: Dogmatic Constitution on the Church *Lumen Gentium*, 11: AAS 57 (1965) 15-16; Pope Paul VI, *Talk on September 15, 1965: Insegnamenti di Paolo VI*, III (1965) 1036.

[167] Cf. Vatican Council II: Constitution on the Sacred Liturgy *Sacrosanctum Concilium*, 47: AAS 56 (1964) 113.

[168] Cf. Pope Paul VI: Encyclical *Mysterium Fidei:* AAS 57 (1965) 553-574.

acuteness of theologians, by men of deep faith and prayer, and by ascetics and mystics, in complete fidelity to the Eucharistic mystery, it still reaches no more than the threshold, since it is incapable of grasping and translating into words what the Eucharist is in all its fullness, what is expressed by it and what is actuated by it. Indeed, the Eucharist is the ineffable Sacrament! The essential commitment and, above all, the visible grace and source of supernatural strength for the Church as the People of God is to persevere and advance constantly in Eucharistic life and Eucharistic piety and to develop spiritually in the climate of the Eucharist. With all the greater reason, then, it is not permissible for us, in thought, life or action, to take away from this truly most holy Sacrament its full magnitude and its essential meaning. It is at one and the same time a Sacrifice-Sacrament, a Communion-Sacrament, and a Presence-Sacrament And, although it is true that the Eucharist always was and must continue to be the most profound revelation of the human brotherhood of Christ's disciples and confessors, it cannot be treated merely as an "occasion" for manifesting this brotherhood. When celebrating the Sacrament of the Body and Blood of the Lord, the full magnitude of the divine mystery must be respected, as must the full meaning of this sacramental sign in which Christ is really present and is received, the soul is filled with grace and the pledge of future glory is given.[169]

This is the source of the duty to carry out rigorously the liturgical rules and everything that is a manifestation of community worship offered to God himself, all the more so because in this sacramental sign he entrusts himself to us with limitless trust, as if not taking into consideration our human weakness, our

---

[169] Cf. Vatican Council II: Constitution on the Sacred Liturgy *Sacrosanctum Concilium*, 47: AAS 56 (1964) 113.

unworthiness, the force of habit, routine, or even the possibility of insult. Every member of the Church, especially Bishops and Priests, must be vigilant in seeing that this Sacrament of love shall be at the centre of the life of the People of God, so that through all the manifestations of worship due to it Christ shall be given back "love for love" and truly become "the life of our souls".[170] Nor can we, on the other hand, ever forget the following words of Saint Paul: "Let a man examine himself, and so eat of the bread and drink of the cup".[171]

This call by the Apostle indicates at least indirectly the close link between the Eucharist and Penance. Indeed, if the first word of Christ's teaching, the first phrase of the Gospel Good News, was "Repent, and believe in the gospel" (*metanoeite*),[172] the Sacrament of the Passion, Cross and Resurrection seems to strengthen and consolidate in an altogether special way this call in our souls. The Eucharist and Penance thus become in a sense two closely connected dimensions of authentic life in accordance with the spirit of the Gospel, of truly Christian life. The Christ who calls to the Eucharistic banquet is always the same Christ who exhorts us to penance and repeats his "Repent".[173] Without this constant ever renewed endeavour for conversion, partaking of the Eucharist would lack its full redeeming effectiveness and there would be a loss or at least a weakening of the special readiness to offer God the spiritual sacrifice[174] in which our sharing in the priesthood of Christ is expressed in an essential and universal manner. In Christ, priesthood is linked with his

---

[170] Cf. Jn 6:51, 57; 14:6; Gal 2:20.

[171] 1 Cor 11:28.

[172] Mk 1:15.

[173] *Ibid.*

[174] Cf. 1 Pt 2:5.

Sacrifice, his self-giving to the Father; and, precisely because it is without limit, that self-giving gives rise in us human beings subject to numerous limitations to the need to turn to God in an ever more mature way and with a constant, ever more profound, conversion.

In the last years much has been done to highlight in the Church's practice—in conformity with the most ancient tradition of the Church—the community aspect of penance and especially of the sacrament of Penance. We cannot however forget that conversion is a particularly profound inward act in which the individual cannot be replaced by others and cannot make the community be a substitute for him. Although the participation by the fraternal community of the faithful in the penitential celebration is a great help for the act of personal conversion, nevertheless, in the final analysis, it is necessary that in this act there should be a pronouncement by the individual himself with the whole depth of his conscience and with the whole of his sense of guilt and of trust in God, placing himself like the Psalmist before God to confess: "Against you . . . have I sinned".[175] In faithfully observing the centuries-old practice of the Sacrament of Penance—the practice of individual confession .with a personal act of sorrow and the intention to amend and make satisfaction—the Church is therefore defending the human soul's individual right: man's right to a more personal encounter with the crucified forgiving Christ, with Christ saying, through the minister of the sacrament of Reconciliation: "Your sins are forgiven";[176] "Go, and do not sin again".[177] As is evident, this is also a right on Christ's part with regard to every human being

---

[175] Ps 50 (51):6.

[176] Mk 2:5.

[177] Jn 8:11.

redeemed by him: his right to meet each one of us in that key moment in the soul's life constituted by the moment of conversion and forgiveness. By guarding the sacrament of Penance, the Church expressly affirms her faith in the mystery of the Redemption as a living and life-giving reality that fits in with man's inward truth, with human guilt and also with the desires of the human conscience. "Blessed are those who hunger and thirst for righteousness, for they shall be satisfied".[178] The sacrament of Penance is the means to satisfy man with the righteousness that comes from the Redeemer himself.

In the Church, gathering particularly today in a special way around the Eucharist and desiring that the authentic Eucharistic community should become a sign of the gradually maturing unity of all Christians, there must a lively-felt need for penance, both in its sacramental aspect,[179] and in what concerns penance as a virtue. This second aspect was expressed by Paul VI in the Apostolic Constitution *Paenitemini*.[180] One of the Church's tasks is to put into practice the teaching *Paenitemini* contains; this subject must be investigated more deeply by us in common reflection, and many more decisions must be made about it in a spirit of pastoral collegiality and with respect for the different traditions in this regard and the different circumstances of the lives of the people of today. Nevertheless, it is certain that the Church of the new Advent, the Church that is continually

---

[178] Mt 5:6.

[179] Cf. Sacred Congregation for the Doctrine of the Faith: *Normae Pastorales circa Absolutionem Sacramentalem Generali Modo Impertiendam:* AAS 64 (1972) 510-514; Pope Paul VI: *Address to a Group of Bishops from the United States of America on their "ad limina" Visit,* April 20, 1978: AAS 70 (1978) 328-332; Pope John Paul II: *Address to a Group of Canadian Bishops on their "ad limina" Visit,* November 17, 1978: AAS 71 (1979) 32-36.

[180] Cf. AAS 58 (1966) 177-198.

preparing for the new coming of the Lord, must be the Church of the Eucharist and of Penance. Only when viewed in this spiritual aspect of her life and activity is she seen to be the Church of the divine mission, the Church *in statu missionis*, as the Second Vatican Council has shown her to be.

21.   *The Christian vocation to service and kingship*

In building up from the very foundations the picture of the Church as the People of God—by showing the threefold mission of Christ himself, through participation in which we become truly God's People—the Second Vatican Council highlighted, among other characteristics of the Christian vocation, the one that can be described as "kingly". To present all the riches of the Council's teaching we would here have to make reference to numerous chapters and paragraphs of the Constitution *Lumen Gentium* and of many other documents by the Council. However, one element seems to stand out in the midst of all these riches: the sharing in Christ's kingly mission, that is to say the fact of rediscovering in oneself and others the special dignity of our vocation that can be described as "kingship". This dignity is expressed in readiness to serve, in keeping with the example of Christ, who "came not to be served but to serve".[181] If, in the light of this attitude of Christ's, "being a king" is truly possible only by "being a servant" then "being a servant" also demands so much spiritual maturity that it must really be described as "being a king". In order to be able to serve others worthily and effectively we must be able to master ourselves, possess the virtues that make this mastery possible. Our sharing in Christ's kingly mission—his "kingly function" (*munus*) is closely linked

---

[181] Mt 20:28.

with every sphere of both Christian and human morality.

In presenting the complete picture of the People of God and recalling the place among that people held not only by priests but also by the laity, not only by the representatives of the Hierarchy but also by those of the Institutes of Consecrated Life, the Second Vatican Council did not deduce this picture merely from a sociological premise. The Church as a human society can of course be examined and described according to the categories used by the sciences with regard to any human society. But these categories are not enough. For the whole of the community of the People of God and for each member of it what is in question is not just a specific "social membership"; rather, for each and every one what is essential is a particular "vocation". Indeed, the Church as the People of God is also—according to the teaching of Saint Paul mentioned above, of which Pius XII reminded us in wonderful terms—"Christ's Mystical Body".[182] Membership in that body has for its source a particular call, united with the saving action of grace. Therefore, if we wish to keep in mind this community of the People of God, which is so vast and so extremely differentiated, we must see first and foremost Christ saying in a way to each member of the community: "Follow me".[183] It is the community of the disciples, each of whom in a different way—at times very consciously and consistently, at other times not very consciously and very inconsistently—is following Christ. This shows also the deeply "personal" aspect and dimension of this society, which, in spite of all the deficiencies of its community life—in the human meaning of this word—is a community precisely because all its members form it together with Christ himself, at least because they bear in their souls the

---

[182] Pope Pius XII: Encyclical *Mystici Corporis:* AAS 35 (1943) 193-248.
[183] Jn 1:43.

indelible mark of a Christian.

The Second Vatican Council devoted very special attention to showing how this "ontological" community of disciples and confessors must increasingly become, even from the "human" point of view, a community aware of its own life and activity. The initiatives taken by the Council in this field have been followed up by the many further initiatives of a synodal, apostolic and organizational kind. We must however always keep in mind the truth that every initiative serves true renewal in the Church and helps to bring the authentic light that is Christ[184] insofar as the initiative is based on adequate awareness of the individual Christian's vocation and of responsibility for this singular, unique and unrepeatable grace by which each Christian in the community of the People of God builds up the Body of Christ. This principle, the key rule for the whole of Christian practice—apostolic and pastoral practice, practice of interior and of social life—must with due proportion be applied to the whole of humanity and to each human being. The Pope too and every Bishop must apply this principle to himself. Priests and religious must be faithful to this principle. It is the basis on which their lives must be built by married people, parents, and women and men of different conditions and professions, from those who occupy the highest posts in society to those who perform the simplest tasks. It is precisely the principle of the "kingly service" that imposes on each one of us, in imitation of Christ's example, the duty to demand of himself exactly what we have been called to, what we have personally obliged ourselves to by God's grace, in order to respond to our vocation. This fidelity to the vocation received from God through Christ involves the joint responsibility for the

---

[184] Cf. Vatican Council II: Dogmatic Constitution on the Church *Lumen Gentium*, 1: AAS 57 (1965) 5.

Church for which the Second Vatican Council wishes to educate all Christians. Indeed, in the Church as the community of the People of God under the guidance of the Holy Spirit's working, each member has "his own special gift", as Saint Paul teaches.[185] Although this "gift" is a personal vocation and a form of participation in the Church's saving work, it also serves others builds the Church and the fraternal communities in the various spheres of human life on earth.

Fidelity to one's vocation, that is to say persevering readiness for "kingly service", has particular significance for these many forms of building, especially with regard to the more exigent tasks, which have more influence on the life of our neighbour and of the whole of society. Married people must be distinguished for fidelity to their vocation, as is demanded by the indissoluble nature of the sacramental institution of marriage. Priests must be distinguished for a similar fidelity to their vocation, in view of the indelible character that the sacrament of Orders stamps on their souls. In receiving this sacrament, we in the Latin Church knowingly and freely commit ourselves to live in celibacy, and each one of us must therefore do all he can, with God's grace, to be thankful for this gift and faithful to the bond that he has accepted for ever. He must do so as married people must, for they must endeavour with all their strength to persevere in their matrimonial union, building up the family community through this witness of love and educating new generations of men and women, capable in their turn of dedicating the whole of their lives to their vocation, that is to say to the "kingly service "of which Jesus Christ has offered us the example and the most beautiful model. His Church, made up of all of us, is "for men"

---

[185] 1 Cor 7:7; cf. 12:7, 27; Rom 12:6; Eph 4:7.

in the sense that, by basing ourselves on Christ's example[186] and collaborating with the grace that he has gained for us, we are able to attain to "being kings", that is to say we are able to produce a mature humanity in each one of us. Mature humanity means full use of the gift of freedom received from the Creator when he called to existence the man made "in his image, after his likeness". This gift finds its full realization in the unreserved giving of the whole of one's human person, in a spirit of the love of a spouse, to Christ and, with Christ, to all those to whom he sends men and women totally consecrated to him in accordance with the evangelical counsels. This is the ideal of the religious life, which has been undertaken by the Orders and Congregations both ancient and recent, and by the Secular Institutes.

Nowadays it is sometimes held, though wrongly, that freedom is an end in itself, that each human being is free when he makes use of freedom as he wishes, and that this must be our aim in the lives of individuals and societies. In reality, freedom is a great gift only when we know how to use it consciously for everything that is our true good. Christ teaches us that the best use of freedom is charity, which takes concrete form in self-giving and in service. For this "freedom Christ has set us free"[187] and ever continues to set us free. The Church draws from this source the unceasing inspiration, the call and the drive for her mission and her service among all mankind. The full truth about human freedom is indelibly inscribed on the mystery of the Redemption. The Church truly serves mankind when she guards this truth with untiring attention, fervent love and mature commitment and when in the whole of her own community she transmits it

---

[186] Cf. Vatican Council II: Dogmatic Constitution on the Church *Lumen Gentium*, 36: AAS 57 (1965) 41-42.

[187] Gal 5:1; cf. 5:13.

and gives it concrete form in human life through each Christian's fidelity to his vocation. This confirms what we have already referred to, namely that man is and always becomes the "way" for the Church's daily life.

22. *The Mother in whom we trust*

When therefore at the beginning of the new pontificate I turn my thoughts and my heart to the Redeemer of man, I thereby wish to enter and penetrate into the deepest rhythm of the Church's life. Indeed, if the Church lives her life, she does so because she draws it from Christ, and he always wishes but one thing, namely that we should have life and have it abundantly.[188] This fullness of life in him is at the same time for man. Therefore the Church, uniting herself with all the riches of the mystery of the Redemption, becomes the Church of living people, living because given life from within by the working of "the Spirit of truth"[189] and visited by the love that the Holy Spirit has poured into our hearts.[190] The aim of any service in the Church, whether the service is apostolic, pastoral, priestly or episcopal, is to keep up this dynamic link between the mystery of the Redemption and every man.

If we are aware of this task, then we seem to understand better what it means to say that the Church is a mother[191] and also what it means to say that the Church always, and particularly at our time, has need of a Mother. We owe a debt of special gratitude to the Fathers of the Second Vatican Council, who

---

[188] Cf. Jn 10:10.

[189] Jn 16:13.

[190] Cf. Rom 5:5.

[191] Cf. Vatican Council II: Dogmatic Constitution on the Church *Lumen Gentium*, 63-64; AAS 57 (1965) 64.

expressed this truth in the Constitution *Lumen Gentium* with the rich Mariological doctrine contained in it.[192] Since Paul VI, inspired by that teaching, proclaimed the Mother of Christ "Mother of the Church",[193] and that title has become known far and wide, may it be permitted to his unworthy Successor to turn to Mary as Mother of the Church at the close of these reflections which it was opportune to make at the beginning of his papal service. Mary is Mother of the Church because, on account of the Eternal Father's ineffable choice[194] and due to the Spirit of Love's special action,[195] she gave human life to the Son of God, "for whom and by whom all things exist"[196] and from whom the whole of the People of God receives the grace and dignity of election. Her Son explicitly extended his Mother's maternity in a way that could easily be understood by every soul and every heart by designating, when he was raised on the Cross, his beloved disciple as her son.[197] The Holy Spirit inspired her to remain in the .Upper Room, after our Lord's Ascension, recollected in prayer and expectation, together with the Apostles, until the day of Pentecost, when the Church was to be born in visible form, coming forth from darkness.[198] Later, all the generations of disciples, of those who confess and love Christ, like the Apostle John, spiritually took this Mother to their own homes,[199] and she

---

[192] Cf. Chapter VIII, 52-69; AAS 57 (1965) 58-67.

[193] Pope Paul VI: *Closing Address at the Third Session of the Second Vatican Ecumenical Council*, November 21, 1964: AAS 56 (1964) 1015.

[194] Cf. Vatican Council II: Dogmatic Constitution on the Church *Lumen Gentium*, 56: AAS 57 (1965) 60.

[195] *Ibid.*

[196] Heb 2:10.

[197] Cf. Jn 19:26.

[198] Cf. Acts 1:14; 2.

[199] Cf. Jn 19:27.

was thus included in the history of salvation and in the Church's mission from the very beginning, that is from the moment of the Annunciation. Accordingly, we who form today's generation of disciples of Christ all wish to unite ourselves with her in a special way. We do so with all our attachment to our ancient tradition and also with full respect and love for the members of all the Christian Communities.

We do so at the urging of the deep need of faith, hope and charity. For if we feel a special need, in this difficult and responsible phase of the history of the Church and of mankind, to turn to Christ, who is Lord of the Church and Lord of man's history on account of the mystery of the Redemption, we believe that nobody else can bring us as Mary can into the divine and human dimension of this mystery. Nobody has been brought into it by God himself as Mary has. It is in this that the exceptional character of the grace of the divine Motherhood consists. Not only is the dignity of this Motherhood unique and unrepeatable in the history of the human race, but Mary's participation, due to this Maternity, in God's plan for man's salvation through the mystery of the Redemption is also unique in profundity and range of action.

We can say that the mystery of the Redemption took shape beneath the heart of the Virgin of Nazareth when she pronounced her "fiat". From then on, under the special influence of the Holy Spirit, this heart, the heart of both a virgin and a mother, has always followed the work of her Son and has gone out to all those whom Christ has embraced and continues to embrace with inexhaustible love. For that reason her heart must also have the inexhaustibility of a mother. The special characteristic of the motherly love that the Mother of God inserts in the mystery of the Redemption and the life of the Church finds expression in its exceptional closeness to man and all that happens to him. It is in this that the mystery of the Mother consists. The Church, which looks to her with altogether special love and hope, wishes to make this mystery her own in an ever deeper manner. For in this the Church also recognizes the way for her daily life, which is each person.

The Father's eternal love, which has been manifested in the history of mankind through the Son whom the Father gave, "that whoever believes in him should not perish but have eternal life",[200] comes close to each of us through this Mother and thus takes on tokens that are of more easy understanding and access by each person. Consequently, Mary must be on all the ways for the Church's daily life. Through her maternal presence the Church acquires certainty that she is truly living the life of her Master and Lord and that she is living the mystery of the Redemption in all its life—giving profundity and fullness. Likewise the Church, which has struck root in many varied fields of the life of the whole of present—day humanity, also acquires the certainty and, one could say, the experience of being close to man, to each person, of being each person's Church, the Church of the People of God.

Faced with these tasks that appear along the ways for the Church, those ways that Pope Paul VI clearly indicated in the first Encyclical of his pontificate, and aware of the absolute necessity of all these ways and also of the difficulties thronging them, we feel all the more our need for a profound link with Christ. We hear within us, as a resounding echo, the words that he spoke: "Apart from me you can do nothing".[201] We feel not only the need but even a categorical imperative for great, intense and growing

---

[200] Jn 3:16.
[201] Jn 15:5.

prayer by all the Church. Only prayer can prevent all these great succeeding tasks and difficulties from becoming a source of crisis and make them instead the occasion and, as it were, the foundation for ever more mature achievements on the People of God's march towards the Promised Land in this stage of history approaching the end of the second millennium. Accordingly, as I end this meditation with a warm and humble call to prayer, I wish the Church to devote herself to this prayer, together with Mary the Mother of Jesus,[202] as the Apostles and disciples of the Lord did in the Upper Room in Jerusalem after his Ascension.[203] Above all, I implore Mary, the heavenly Mother of the Church, to be so good as to devote herself to this prayer of humanity's new Advent, together with us who make up the Church, that is to say the Mystical Body of her Only Son. I hope that through this prayer we shall be able to receive the Holy Spirit coming upon us[204] and thus become Christ's witnesses "to the end of the earth",[205] like those who went forth from the Upper Room in Jerusalem on the day of Pentecost.

With the Apostolic Blessing.

Given at Rome, at Saint Peter's, on the fourth of March, the First Sunday of Lent, in the year 1979, the first year of my Pontificate.

☦ **JOHN PAUL II** ☦

---

[202] Cf. Acts 1:14.
[203] Cf. Acts 1:13.
[204] Cf. Acts 1:8.
[205] *Ibid.*

Book Catalog

Works by Our Authors

- *The Opium of Happiness* by Jeremy Hausotter. This book examines the Church's teachings on drugs and marijuana. It also contains about 70 pages of appendices of hard to find Church documents discussing drugs. ISBN: 978-1-964170-54-1

- *How to Win Tic Tac Toe Like a Champion* by Jeremy Hausotter. ISBN: 978-1-964170-58-9

Theology & Philosophy

- *Select Works* by **St. Ambrose**. ISBN: 978-1-964170-44-2

- **St. Thomas Aquinas**

    - *The Summa Theologiae: Prima Pars, Q. 1-119.* ISBN: 978-1-964170-23-7

    - *The Summa Theologiae: Prima Secundae, Q. 1-114.* ISBN: 978-1-964170-24-4

    - *The Summa Theologiae: Secunda Secundae, Q. 1-189.* ISBN: 978-1-964170-25-1

    - *The Summa Theologiae: Tertia Pars, Q. 1-90.* ISBN: 978-1-964170-27-5

    - *The Summa Theologiae: Supplementum, Q. 1-99.* ISBN: 978-1-964170-28-2

- *The Life of St. Anthony* by **St. Athanasius**. ISBN: 978-1-964170-20-6

- **St. Augustine**

    - *Select Doctrinal Treatises, and Moral Treatises* ISBN: 978-1-964170-63-3

    - *The Anti-Donatist Works.* ISBN: 978-1-964170-40-4

    - *The Anti-Manichean Works.* ISBN: 978-1-964170-67-1

    - *The Anti-Pelagian Works.* ISBN: 978-1-964170-65-7

- *The Art of Dying Well* by **St. Robert Bellarmine**. ISBN: 978-1-964170-62-6

- *Select Letters and Orations* by **St. Gregory Nazianzen**. ISBN: 978-1-964170-56-5

- **St. John Henry Newman**

  - *An Essay in Aid of a Grammar of Assent.* ISBN: 978-1-964170-52-7

  - *The Complete Parochial and Plain Sermons*, volumes 1–4. ISBN: 978-1-964170-22-0

  - *The Complete Parochial and Plain Sermons*, volumes 5–8. ISBN: 978-1-964170-66-4

  - *The Complete Historical Sketches*, volumes 1–3. ISBN: 978-1-964170-71-8

  - *On the Development of Christian Doctrine.* ISBN: 978-1-964170-48-0

  - *Sermons Preached on Various Occasions.* ISBN: 978-1-964170-50-3

- *The Problem of Form in Painting and Sculpture* by **Adolf von Hildebrand**. ISBN: 978-1-964170-60-2

Papal Documents

- **The Papal Writings of John Paul II**

  - Vol. 1, *The Complete Encyclicals.* ISBN: 978-1-964170-21-3

  - Vol. 2, *Redemptor Hominis.* ISBN: 978-1-964170-00-8

  - Vol. 3, *Dives in Misericordia.* ISBN: 978-1-964170-01-5

  - Vol. 4, *Laborem Exercens.* ISBN: 978-1-964170-02-2

  - Vol. 11, *Veritatis Splendor.* ISBN: 978-1-964170-09-1

  - Vol. 12, *Evangelium Vitae.* ISBN: 978-1-964170-10-7

  - Vol. 14, *Fides et Ratio.* ISBN: 978-1-964170-12-1

- **The Papal Writings of Benedict XVI**

  - Vol. 1, *Select Papal Writings: The Encyclicals, Apostolic Exhortations, and Select Other Writings.* ISBN: 978-1-964170-14-5

Classics

- **The Complete Works of Fyodor Dostoevsky**

    - Vol. 8, *The Minor Novels and Novellas: The Insulted and the Injured, The House of the Dead.* ISBN: 978-1-964170-17-6

    - Vol. 9, *The Complete Short Stories.* ISBN: 978-1-964170-18-3

- *The Wind in the Willows* by **Kenneth Grahame**.
  ISBN: 978-1-964170-46-6

- **Greek and Roman Classics**

    - Vol. 1, *Homer's The Iliad and the Odyssey,* translated by Alexander Pope. ISBN: 978-1-964170-15-2

    - Vol. 4, *Commentaries* by Julius Caesar. ISBN: 978-1-964170-72-5

- **Norse Classics**

    - Vol. 1, *The Poetic and Prose Eddas.* ISBN: 978-1-964170-37-4

    - Vol. 2, *The Heimskringla.* ISBN: 978-1-964170-39-8

    - Vol. 3, *The Nibelungenlied* (prose translation).
      ISBN: 978-1-964170-33-6

    - Vol. 4, *The Norse Sagas, Part 1.* ISBN: 978-1-964170-35-0

    - Vol. 5, *The Norse Sagas, Part 2.* ISBN: 978-1-964170-29-9

    - Vol. 6, *The Norse Sagas, Part 3.* ISBN: 978-1-964170-31-2

- *20,000 Leagues Under the Sea* by **Jules Verne**.
  ISBN: 978-1-964170-42-8

Forthcoming Titles

- A volume on the dogma *no salvation outside of the Church* by Jeremy Hausotter.

- A volume on the hermeneutics of Vatican II by Jeremy Hausotter.

- The *Summa Contra Gentiles* by St. Thomas Aquinas.